Empowering Children to Help STOP Bullying at School

A curriculum for grades **three and up**

CAROL WINTLE

Empowering Children to Help Stop Bullying at School:
A curriculum for grades three and up by Carol Wintle

Publisher: Character Development Group, Inc.
366 Bella Vista Dr., Boone, NC 28607
Toll-free: 888.262.0572
E-mail: Info@CharacterEducation.com
www.CharacterEducation.com

ISBN: 978-1-892056-54-2 $24.95
Library of Congress Control Number: 2009931540

Printed in the United States of America

for the children

And thanks to
Peyton, Lila, Sue,
Ross, Veronica, Lani, Kaia, Mary,
Elizabeth, Susan, Elest, Cecile, Gabby,
Suzi, Sammy, Jane, Elisa, D.J., Carolyn, Andrew
Catherine A., Catherine B., Sarah, Jared, Alicia, and Larry
for playing an important role in the shaping of this book.

CONTENTS

INTRODUCTION

My journey toward the creation of *Empowering Children to Help Stop Bullying at School* probably began when I was a child and bullied by a girl who lived in my neighborhood. That early life experience sensitized me to the needs of children who find themselves in similar circumstances.

As an educator and psychotherapist, I have helped many children who were bullied, observers of bullying, and the ones doing the bullying. In the early 1990's I was hired as a Coordinator of Conflict Resolution Programs for a local educational organization. While being trained by a conflict resolution expert, I noticed that many teachers told stories of student problems that could not be solved by standard conflict resolution. What they were talking about was bullying.

The following year, in a brainstorming session to come up with new workshops the organization could offer, I thought of the title *Bullies and Scapegoats*. My co-workers encouraged me to create such a workshop. Attempting to succeed at this task I researched the topic and discovered the groundbreaking book *Bullying at school: What we know and what we can do* by Norwegian researcher and professor of psychology, Dan Olweus.

Armed with the knowledge of Mr. Olweus's research and his whole school *Bullying Prevention Plan*, I designed and presented workshops for school staff, counselors and parents on bullying prevention at school. I researched children's literature on the topic of bullying and learned that many authors showed solutions that involved tricking or physical fighting with the children who bully. This led me to compile a bibliography of books that promoted only assertive actions.

With the help of an Anita L. Mishler Education Fund Fellowship grant the bibliography grew into a middle school curriculum called *Stop Bullying at School*. Concurrently I wrote an early childhood guide called "Preventing Name-calling and Bullying" which was published in *Adventures in Peacemaking: A Conflict Resolution Activity Guide for Early Childhood Providers*.

Subsequently, I performed storytelling and puppet shows, and led classes on the topic of bullying for elementary school audiences. I looked for a story that showed a range of assertive techniques upper elementary students could use to stick up for themselves and others. In the past ten years the educational market has exploded with resources on bullying. Despite the wealth of materials now available, I could not find what I was looking for. So I created the story of Avery Quinn, which forms the core of *Empowering Children to Help Stop Bullying at School*.

BULLYING AT SCHOOL

Bullying is when one person or a group of people who are more powerful (stronger, older, more skilled, or more popular) intentionally treats someone disrespectfully over and over again.

Bullying at school is substantial and merits serious attention. Studies done in the United States conclude that one or two of every ten students at school are bullied. Include the children who bully and those who silently watch bullying at school and the number of students affected by bullying could be as high as 95% or more.

Other research findings support this concept. The following statistics apply to the United States.

- 80% of 250 young people surveyed reported that they liked to tease to make someone else miserable.
- 43% of students surveyed said they were afraid to go to a bathroom at school because of harassment.
- Every day in America over 160,000 children miss school because they are afraid of being bullied.
- 8% of students miss school one day a month because they are afraid of being bullied.
- Verbal bullying is the most common form of bullying; physical bullying the least common.
- Name-calling is the most common type of bullying tactic used by children of all ages.
- Peers are present in 85% of bullying episodes, but only intervene to stop bullying 10% of the time.
- Less than a third of students surveyed said they report bullying to school staff.

- In a national survey of students in grades 6-10, 13% reported bullying others, 11% reported being the targets of bullies, and another 6% said that they bullied others and were bullied themselves.
- Those who are frequently teased in childhood are more likely to suffer from depression and anxiety as adults.
- 60% of boys who were characterized as bullies in grades 6-9 had been convicted of a least one officially registered crime by the age of 24.

Bullying, which impacts student attendance and the ability to perform, can also affect a child's desire to live and their personal safety at school. Painful, on-going bullying has influenced young people's decisions to commit suicide or school shootings. Prolonged bullying at school, which commonly starts in preschool or elementary school, can lead to tragedies later on that might have been prevented.

The key to bullying prevention is in shifting the "silent majority" into a "caring majority."

Garrity, C., Jens, K., Porter, W., Sager, N., and Short-Camilli, C. *Bully-proofing your school: A comprehensive approach for elementary schools*, Sopris West, 2000.

- Bullycide is defined as a suicide caused as the result of depression from bullying. 11-year-old Carl Joseph Walker-Hoover from Springfield, Massachusetts killed himself after being repeatedly bullied by students at the New Leadership Charter School who called Carl *gay, fag, queer,* and *homo.* 11-year-old Jaheem Herrera from Atlanta, Georgia killed himself after relentless anti-gay bullying by students at Dunaire Elementary School. These suicides which occurred in April of 2009 are believed to be examples of an extensive world-wide problem of bullycide.

- 71% of school shooters felt that, before they became violent, they had been targets of longstanding and severe threats, attacks, injury, persecution, and bullying.

- Popular students at school who called him nerd teased Evan Ramsey from Bethel Alaska for years. In 1997 Evan shot and killed a fellow student and his high school principal and injured two more students.

- Eric Harris and Dylan Klebold from Littleton, Colorado were long-time targets of bullying. One incident in particular happened in the school cafeteria where students surrounded Eric and Dylan, called them *faggots,* laughed, and squirted ketchup on them. In 1999 Eric and Dylan shot and killed thirteen students, before killing themselves. Eric is quoted as saying, "This is what you get for the way you treated us." His e-mail suicide note said, "Your children who have ridiculed me, who have chosen not to accept me, who have treated me like I am not worth their time are dead."

• Andy Williams from Santee, California, a long-time target of bullying was teased by his classmates because he had big ears and was short. Students stole his belongings including his shoes and two skateboards. They called him *freak, dork, nerd, skinny faggot,* and *gay.* They slammed him against a tree, beat him up, and frequently burned his neck by spraying hairspray on it and lighting the hairspray on fire with a cigarette lighter. In an e-mail message to a friend, Andy wrote that he was fearful to go to school. The following weekend at a sleepover, an adult who heard Andy boast of having a plan to kill kids at his school told Andy that if he ever said things like that again, he'd turn him into the police. Andy said he was just kidding. The next day, Andy shot and killed two fellow high school students, and injured thirteen more schoolmates and two adults (2001).

• Another teenager from Pearl High School in Mississippi killed two fellow students and wounded seven others. He told Secret Service agents that he "felt like nobody cared. I just didn't have anyone to talk to about all the things I was going through. I kept a lot of hurt inside me."

> **...children who bully need to be exposed to prosocial peers who can model positive behavior and help send a message that bullying is not acceptable behavior.**
>
> Kowalski, Limber, and Agatston. *Cyber Bullying: Bullying in the Digital Age,* Blackwell Publishing, 2008.

Bullying occurs in pre-school through grade 12. Why would a five-year-old seek to overpower a classmate and intentionally treat him or her with disrespect over and over again? In the 1970's Dan Olweus asked himself a similar question and sought to find the answer. His research grew into the first large-scale scientific study of bullying that had ever been done. Since then numerous research teams throughout the world have built on Olweus's original findings.

There are children who initiate bullying and those that follow the initiators. It is believed that the initiators, or leaders of bullying, *often* come from homes where a primary caretaker in the child's early years:

• is limited in their ability to offer warmth and emotional nurturing,

• is too permissive and not able to set limits on the child's behavior, and

• at times uses harsh discipline with physical punishment and/or verbally aggressive outbursts.

Students with this kind of early childhood background develop hostile feelings, impulsive/aggressive behavior, and a compulsive need to dominate, control, over-power and make others suffer.

The children they bully often have anxious, quiet, cautious and sensitive personalities, are insecure, and when bullied react emotionally and withdraw. In addition, they do not get help from other students who support the children who bully instead by joining in with them or silently watching and do nothing to help.

To reverse this trend, we can encourage all students to be helpers for those in need. Helpers stick up for or befriend children who are bullied and enlist the assistance of adults. To be a good helper children need to feel confident in their ability to assert themselves.

It is common for students when treated with disrespect to respond passively or with aggression. Assertiveness is a skill of self-control that requires instruction. As with learning to read or play a musical instrument, youth need to see the skill modeled and have many opportunities to practice and receive feedback in order to master the skill.

This curriculum helps you teach children how to:

- assertively handle disrespect from peers,
- work with adults to stop bullying at school, and
- feel empowered to change their behavior if they bully, are bullied, or silently watch.

Success of this program can be measured by a reversal of status with those who are bullied gaining social status and those who choose to bully lose support for doing so. Also evident would be a decrease in silent observers and an increase in helpers.

> **It must become "uncool" to bully, "cool" to help our kids who are bullied and normative for staff and students to notice when a child is bullied or left out.**
>
> Health Resources and Services Administration, 2006.

HOW TO USE THIS CURRICULUM

Ten sections

Empowering Children to Help Stop Bullying at School is divided into ten sections. Each section contains objectives, activities, and handouts. The first eight sections of the curriculum begin with the teacher reading aloud a chapter or two of *Avery Quinn*. The chapters are short and take approximately five to ten minutes to read. Each of the eight sections also contains a focused topic including: What Is Bullying?, Respect & Disrespect, Who Bullies?, Who Is Bullied?, Who Silently Watches Bullying?, Who Are the Helpers?, Tragedy & Courage, and Stop Bullying at School.

Section nine of the curriculum focuses on Jackie Robinson, how he was bullied, how he coped with it, and how he was helped. In section ten, students read books, stories and essays on bullying and present written and oral reports.

The story of Avery Quinn

Avery Quinn's schoolmates bully him and silently watch him being bullied. An adult teaches Avery a variety of ways he can assertively stick up for himself and gives him opportunities to practice each of these techniques. Avery's father helps as well. Gradually over time, Avery learns how to assert himself. Some students who joined in on the bullying or had silently watched Avery being bullied end up helping him instead.

The focus in *Avery Quinn* is primarily on verbal harassment. Adults in the story do not directly intervene with the students who bully so that a range of ways to deal with verbal harassment can be shown.

The story is used to teach all students how to assertively respond when treated with disrespect. It shows them ways to stop supporting bullying and how to help stop it instead.

Objectives

The Core Objectives of this curriculum are to:

• provide students with a definition and examples of bullying,

• introduce the concepts of passive, aggressive, and assertive behavior,

• provide children with a wide-variety of illustrations of how they can assertively stick up for themselves when treated with disrespect,

- identify characteristics of helpers,
- introduce and explore the concept of sticking up for others and the powerful role helpers play in stopping bullying at school,
- provide opportunities for students to develop their assertive communication skills, and
- explore ways students can help stop bullying at school.

Additional objectives are to:
- explore the concepts of respect and disrespect,
- identify the difference between those who lead the bullying and those that follow,
- identify behaviors of those who are bullied,
- identify characteristics of students who silently watch bullying and the role they play in encouraging bullying,
- introduce the concept of *Respect Agreements,*
- explore ways to successfully keep *Respect Agreements,*
- provide information on the seriousness of bullying and the importance of children and adults working together to stop bullying at school,
- involve students in creatively illustrating examples of assertive communication through a variety of art forms such as poems, stories, puppet shows, skits, cartoons and posters, and
- provide information on an historical example of bullying and the role that helpers, assertiveness, and courage played in overcoming bullying.

Activities & Handouts

The activities and handouts in this book respond to the read-aloud sections as well as the focused topics. Activities include discussions, role-plays and skits, creating *Respect Agreements, Respect Meetings,* art projects, journal writing and homework.

Other

If time is limited you can cover the basics of this curriculum in the following way:
- read aloud the entire *Avery Quinn* story (approximately 1½ hours),
- present information on *Respect and Disrespect, What Is Bullying?, Who Silently Watches Bullying?, Who Are the Helpers?, Tragedy & Courage,* and *Stop Bullying at School,*
- conduct follow-up *Discussions,*
- involve students in *Stick Up for Yourself* and *Stick Up for Others* Role-plays,
- assign **Homework** and **Journal** reflections.

All of the above will be highlighted by **bold type** in the first eight Sections of this book. Especially important handouts to include are the ones titled *Troy, Amy, Lauren, Slater, Guivens, Christina, Holly, Latoya, Crystal, Todd,* and *Marissa* in section Seven and *Nelson* in section Eight.

Before you use this curriculum spend time yourself reflecting on...

1. Times when your peers or superiors treated you with disrespect.

2. How did you feel?

3. Did you respond with passive, assertive or aggressive behavior?

4. Times when you observed one adult or a group of adults disrespecting another adult.

5. How did you feel?

6. Was your response passive, assertive, or aggressive?

7. When your response was assertive, what did you do to calm yourself?

As adults we need to *walk our talk* and not expect children to do anything that we ourselves wouldn't do.

Empowering Children to Help Stop Bullying at School is meant to be used as part of a more comprehensive bullying prevention plan that:

- provides support for children who are bullied as well as those that help them,

- provides good supervision throughout the school,

- uses non–hostile, caring consequences consistently when students behavior is unacceptable,

- maintains nurturing relationships with all students, including those who bully,

- praises students' kind actions,

- involves not only teaching staff but non-teaching staff, administrators, and parents, and

- provides training in effective bullying prevention intervention.

For more information on what school personnel and parents can do to help stop bullying at school see the *Resources* section of this text.

NE

What Is Bullying?

Objective
To provide students with a definition and examples of bullying.

Chapter Summary, *Avery Quinn: Unnatural Disasters*

Avery, a fourth grader is bullied by a group of students at his school. Avery is the narrator who shows us what happens and what he thinks and feels.

Suggestions for Success

The following approach is recommended to help prevent students who bully from disrupting classroom activities.

1. Skillfully manage your own feelings so you can maintain a calm demeanor.

2. Treat all the children in your group in a nurturing way, even those who are disruptive.

3. Praise students' kind and respectful behaviors.

4. Provide a choice and consequence for those who choose to be disruptive. For example, they can choose to act respectful and stay with their classmates or they will have to leave until the activity is over.

5. When students continue to disrupt, enforce this consequence in a calm, firm, and caring manner. Send them to the place you have pre-arranged for them to be.

6. When the activity is over, the students who were disruptive return to your class. Greet them in a positive manner.

7. Continue to use this approach to help motivate students to act in a way that will allow them to stay with their class.

Activities

Avery Quinn: Unnatural Disasters

    a. Read the chapter aloud to the class.

    b. Utilize the Chapter Discusion guestions to promote conversation about the chapter.

Select from the recommended activities below, especially those in bold.

1. **Homework: *Feelings* and *What Is Bullying?***

    a. Distribute the Handouts: *Feelings* and *What Is Bullying?* for each child to complete and turn in.

2. Sammy and Claire: examples of bullying.

    a. Divide the class into groups.

    b. Give each group one example of bullying, either Sammy or Claire.

    c. After students complete the handouts, reconvene. Ask children to share their answers for the examples Claire and Sammy. At the end of the activity students turn in their work.

3. **Homework: *Interview—What Is Bullying?***

    a. Students interview a family member, friend, neighbor, or teacher about bullying and complete the Handout: *Interview—What Is Bullying?*

    b. In small groups students compare their interview results, and when they are done, turn in their work.

4. **Journal**

Students respond to the following questions in their journals.

    a. How is Avery feeling?

    b. Why are Ryon and Carlos mean to him?

    c. Could something similar happen at our school? Explain your answer.

    d. Why doesn't Avery have friends?

    e. Why didn't he tell his father about being bullied?

Avery Quinn: *Unnatural Disasters*

My head and stomach ached as I limped to the bus stop my first day of fourth grade. I was sweating. It felt more like summer than fall. My skin itched unbearably where my leg brace rubbed against my knee. I wished I were still on vacation, my bare feet in the Nashua River.

I saw the school bus coming. My chest tightened. *A lion's cage on wheels!* I thought. I quickly shoved my ugly hand into my pocket to hide it. The doors opened. I climbed the steps, putting my right foot on the first step and pulling my left leg up. Then the right foot on the second step, followed by pulling up the left. Without looking at anyone around me I slumped into the only front seat on the bus. That is where I always sat. Alone.

"If it isn't the sportsman Avery Quinn," a mean and familiar voice yelled from the back of the bus.

My hot body went instantly cold.

"Avery is a girl," the boy shouted.

It was Ryon. He knew I was a boy but teased me about my name.

"Pirate, where's your hook?" he called.

I couldn't hear anyone else on the bus talking, only Ryon.

"Sit with us," he yelled.

My body was like a block of ice, unable to think or move.

"Too chicken?"

I stared at my clenched fist.

"You still don't know how to speak?"

I thought, *why couldn't this year be different?*

"Are you deaf or just dumb?"

My block of ice cracked. I looked out the window and imagined I saw a volcano. Ryon was standing on its rim screaming for help. He lost his balance and fell headfirst into the scorching lava below.

When we arrived at school the bus driver told me to get off first. I climbed down the stairs one step at a time. The kids behind me seemed like horses charging out of a barn. As soon as my feet touched the ground they galloped past, almost knocking me down. I looked at the crowd of students in front of the school, hoping I'd see a friendly face. But instead, I saw Carlos. A searing pain shot through my left leg.

"Welcome," said Carlos, smiling his big white grin. He had the longest eyelashes I've ever seen a boy have. They looked even longer than they had the year before. He turned to the girls next to him and winked, "Aren't you glad Avery's back?"

I was like a trapped animal, unable to escape.

Ryon caught up to us. I was surprised to see that he had dyed his hair orange. I thought, *his parents must let him do whatever he wants.* He was wearing a blue and gray soccer shirt. His face looked like it always did, flushed and angry.

"I like your hair," one of the girls said to Ryon.

"What's wrong with him?" Ryon asked, pointing a finger at me.

"What's wrong with you?" Carlos asked me.

They had done this routine a thousand times. The girls laughed. It hurt that they thought Carlos was so funny when he picked on me.

Carlos motioned for me to stand in front of him. Not knowing what else I could do, I complied. He towered over me. My block of ice melted. I thought, *if only I could evaporate and disappear.*

"Hurry up," Ryon said. "You're slowing us down."

"Baby steps," jeered Carlos.

My body shivered.

"Quavery Avery," teased Ryon.

"Avery Bravery," joked Carlos.

"Quivery Ivery," said someone else.

I recognized the voice as Enzo's. Last year in

third grade he and his cousin Marcella started hanging around with Ryon and Carlos.

"Quivery Ivery," echoed Marcella.

I passed by the hall monitors who were holding the school doors open.

Ryon and Carlos stuck their tongues out at me as they climbed the stairs to the fifth grade classrooms on the second floor.

Another year of torture, I thought, *how am I going to survive?* I headed for the west wing of the first floor. Enzo walked on one side of me, Marcella on the other.

"What did you do this summer?" asked Enzo. "Run marathons?"

Marcella sprinted ahead. "Catch me if you can," she said.

I stared at the newly polished wood floor. *What a loser,* I told myself, *letting a third grade girl push me around.*

A teacher grabbed Marcella. "No running," she said. "Inside feet, remember?"

"Time to be in your classes," announced the Principal, Mrs. Shane.

Fortunately Enzo and I were in separate rooms.

I collapsed into my assigned desk, turned toward the classroom window, and slipped back into my fantasy world. Outside Marcella was caught in a windstorm. She beat the air with her chubby arms and kicked her short legs with all her force, but the wind was stronger and blew her away.

Then came Enzo gripping tiny poles and skiing down a gigantic snow-covered mountain yelling, "Look at me." He didn't see the avalanche that sped towards him. A few seconds later he was buried under hundreds of feet of snow.

Carlos walked across a field on a warm summer night. Suddenly the sky grew dark. Rain poured down. Lightning, brighter than his smile shot across the sky. Thunder cracked. Louder and louder. Lightning flashed again and zapped Carlos into oblivion.

Chapter Discussion

Discuss *Avery Quinn: Unnatural Disasters.* Ask students not to use children's real names during this discussion. Advise them to communicate privately later if they need to.

1. How is Avery being treated?

2. How does he respond?

3. Why are some students mean to him?

4. Describe a situation where someone was teased because they had a physical handicap or because his or her name was different?

Empowering Children to Help Stop Bullying at School

FEELINGS

Circle the words below that describe how you think Avery is feeling.

Angry	Discouraged	Happy	Possessive
Annoyed	Dissatisfied	Hopeful	Proud
Anxious	Distrustful	Irritated	Peaceful
Apprehensive	Edgy	Jealous	Revengeful
Cautious	Enraged	Joyful	Sad
Cheerful	Excited	Lonely	Satisfied
Concerned	Fearful	Loving	Scared
Confident	Frightened	Mad	Sorrowful
Confused	Frustrated	Miserable	Stressed
Content	Fulfilled	Nervous	Tense
Dejected	Furious	Panicky	Terrified
Delighted	Gloomy	Patient	Unhappy
Depressed	Glum	Pleased	Uptight
	Grateful		Worried

WHAT IS BULLYING?

Bullying is when one person or a group of people who are more powerful (stronger, older, more skilled, or more popular) intentionally treat someone disrespectfully over and over again.

1. How does this definition of bullying fit with what Avery is experiencing?

_____

_____

_____

_____

2. After listening to *Avery Quinn: Unnatural Disasters*, what do you think about each of the characters?

a. Avery _____

_____

b. Ryon _____

_____

c. Carlos_____

_____

d. Enzo _____

_____

e. Marcella _____

_____

3. What do you think about how this chapter opens and how it ends?

_____

_____

_____

_____

SAMMY

Bullying is when one person or a group of people who are more powerful (stronger, older, more skilled, or more popular) intentionally treat someone disrespectfully over and over again.

An older kid at school is always picking on me. When he sees me in the boys bathroom he wrestles me to the floor and tries to pull my pants down. —Sammy, third grade

1. Does Sammy's experience fit with the definition of bullying? If yes, why? If no, why not?

_____

_____

_____

_____

2. What choices does Sammy have to help solve his problem?

_____

_____

_____

_____

3. If you saw someone treated the way Sammy was treated what would you do?

_____

_____

_____

_____

4. Is it ever okay to treat someone the way Sammy was treated? Explain your answer.

_____

_____

_____

_____

CLAIRE

Bullying is when one person or a group of people who are more powerful (stronger, older, more skilled, or more popular) intentionally treat someone disrespectfully over and over again.

Claire was a new student at my school. Two girls started a club against her called the Hate Claire Club. They passed around a note asking us to promise to hate Claire. Almost every girl in the fifth grade signed it. —Jalessa, fifth grade

1. Is it ever okay to treat someone the way Claire was treated? Explain your answer.

_____

_____

_____

_____

2. How does Claire's experience fit with the definition of bullying?

_____

_____

_____

_____

3. What do you think Claire should do?

_____

_____

_____

_____

4. If this happened to someone you knew, what would you do?

_____

_____

_____

_____

INTERVIEW—WHAT IS BULLYING?

A. Interview a family member, friend, neighbor, or teacher to find out what they know about bullying. Record their answers.

Ask the person:

1. What is bullying? Record the answer:

_____

_____

_____

_____

_____

_____

_____

_____

2. Give an example of bullying. Record the example:

_____

_____

_____

_____

_____

_____

_____

_____

Circle the correct description of the person you interviewed.

Family member: mother   father   sister   brother   grandparent   aunt   uncle   other

              friend   neighbor   teacher

TW

Respect & Disrespect

Objectives

- To introduce the concepts of passive, aggressive, and assertive behavior.

- To explore the concepts of respect and disrespect.

- To provide students with a wide variety of illustrations of how they can assertively stick up for themselves when treated with disrespect.

- To help students develop assertive communication skills.

- To explore the concept of bullying.

Chapter Summaries, *Avery Quinn: Rumblings* and *Avery Quinn: Rescue*

Avery Quinn: Rumblings provides background information on Avery and his family.

In *Avery Quinn: Rescue,* Avery's father signs a permission form for Mr. Sergio, the new gym teacher, to provide the extra help his handicapped son is legally entitled to. Mr. Sergio tells Avery he saw children bullying him. Avery promises to tell his father about being picked on. Mr. Sergio attempts to help Avery feel more confident about himself.

Suggestions for Success

1. If a student in your class is repeatedly treated with disrespect, provide that child with support.

2. Try to skillfully manage your own feelings so you can maintain calm.

3. Ask kind and popular students to help out by being friendly to the child.

4. Continue to use consequences that curtail the freedom of those who are unkind.

5. Develop and maintain nurturing relationships with all the children in your group, including those who act mean.

6. Help all your students develop assertiveness skills.

7. Praise students for kind behavior.

8. Involving students in your class in as many of the role-plays in this curriculum as possible is crucial if you want them to be able to actually use these skills at school.

Activities

Avery Quinn: Rumblings and *Rescue*

a. Read the two chapters aloud to the class.

b. Use the Chapter Discussion questions to stimulate a class conversation on the chapters.

Select from the recommended activities below, especially those in bold.

1. Role-play: Speak Up for Yourself #1

Involve either small groups or the whole class in role-plays. Use approach a or b.

a. Divide students into pairs. Distribute the Handout *Speak Up for Yourself #1.*

  • Explain that one student will read the disrespectful statements and the other will pretend to be Avery speaking up for himself. Everyone speaking as Avery should stand tall, pull their shoulders back, hold their head high, and talk calmly without yelling.

  • After students have completed a role-play once, they switch places. The one who played Avery first then reads the disrespectful statement and vice versa.

  • When they are done, students de-brief. They call each other by their real names and ask each other how it felt to read the disrespectful and assertive statements.

b. A simpler way to do this activity, and if the group needs more structure, is for the teacher to read the disrespectful statements and one at a time, or the whole group together, give the assertive responses.

  • When you are done, de-brief. Call students by their real names and ask them how it felt to say the assertive responses.

2. Homework: Speak Up for Yourself #2

a. Give students the Handouts: *Speak Up for Yourself #1* and *#2*

b. Children repeat the *Speak Up for Yourself #1* activity with a family member, friend, neighbor, or teacher and complete the Handout: *Speak Up for Yourself #2.*

3. Respect & Disrespect

a. Divide students into small groups. Give each group one copy of the Handout: *Respect & Disrespect* to complete.

b. Use the *Discussion: Respect & Disrespect* questions to help groups present their responses to the Handout: *Respect & Disrespect.*

c. Collect the handouts and compile a Master list that includes ideas from each of the groups. Save the Master *Respect & Disrespect* list to use in section Three.

4. Practice Observation

a. Distribute the Handout: *Practice Observation.* With the whole class, brainstorm five actions that the class has seen happen at school. Decide which actions are respectful and which are disrespectful and mark each action as R or D accordingly.

Empowering Children to Help Stop Bullying at School

5. Homework: One-Day Observation

a. Distribute the Handout: *One-Day Observation*. Students record five actions that they see or hear, note the time of day and identify each as respectful or disrespectful. Instruct students to refrain from using people's real names. Students turn in their completed handouts.

6. Homework: Two-Day Observation

a. Distribute the Handout: *Two-Day Observation* for students to record actions, dates, and time of day, and to mark whether the actions are respectful or disrespectful.

b. Students orally report the results of their observations to the class. Instruct children to not use people's real names. At the conclusion of this activity students turn in their completed handouts.

7. Don't Laugh at Me

On the website www.operationrespect.org the song "Don't Laugh at Me" is performed by three different musicians, Peter Yarrow, Christine Evans, and Baby Jay. Play these songs for your class prior to the following exercise.

8. Dealing with Disrespect

The Handouts: *Natel, Michael,* and *Zhongmei* are essays, or part of an essay, that sixth graders in the Boston Public Schools, Boston, MA wrote about their experiences of being treated with disrespect.

—*Natel* chose not to be in a group that was cool, yet disrespectful.

—*Michael* is bullied by another boy and successfully stands up for himself.

—*Zhongmei* is asked disrespectful questions about why she was adopted.

a. Distribute one of the three handouts to each student or group to read and complete.

b. Conduct a class discussion of the assignment. Ask volunteers to tell the stories of Natel, Michael, and Zhongmei and share their answers to the questions on the handouts. Afterwards they turn in their completed work.

9. Journal

Students respond to the following questions in their journals.

a. If you were bullied, which adults in your life would you tell? Why?

b. Explain the difference between passive, assertive and aggressive behavior?

c. Write about a time you were treated with disrespect. Describe how you felt.

d. Write about a time you were treated with respect. Describe how you felt.

Avery Quinn: *Rumblings*

When I was born my left foot and hand were so bent I had to have surgery. Now I can walk, but I have to wear a brace on my leg when I go to school. Fortunately, it is hidden underneath my pants. My left hand got fixed so that my fingers are only a little bent, but I still can't move them.

I live with my father. My mom died in a car accident when I was three years old. I don't remember much about her. Pictures in our living room show my father and her laughing with their friends. My father doesn't do that anymore, laugh or have friends.

After the accident he moved us away from everyone he had known, bought the Book Nook bookstore in Lemonburg, Massachusetts, and changed its name to Quinn's Books. He also bought a fancy log cabin surrounded by trees. That's where we lived at the edge of town.

I loved it at the cabin. My father built me forts in the woods where I pretended to be Robin Hood in the Sherwood Forest. All the creatures that lived on our land fascinated me: weasels, racoons, foxes, frogs, rabbits, birds, chipmunks, squirrels, coyote, and deer. The Nashua River flowed along the edge of our property. I spent a lot of time there wading, skipping stones, piling rocks, floating on a raft, swimming, canoeing, fishing and acting like I was the shipwrecked sailor, Robinson Crusoe.

When we weren't at the cabin I was with my father at Quinn Books. I didn't go to kindergarten or first grade. My father home-schooled me. After he taught me how to read he gave me tons of books to read and had me answer thousands of questions about what I had learned.

Even though my father talked to customers all week, he was a loner. I was a loner too. But I didn't want to be. I asked Dad to find me some friends but he never got around to it. I guessed that the only way I could get any was to go to school.

Having just read the book Miss Rumphias, I told my father, "I want a lady teacher."

He thought I was joking.

"I have to go to school," I told him.

"You go to school," he said.

"School where kids are," I protested.

I talked about school every day until finally he said I could go.

But it wasn't what I had expected. On my first day at Parker Elementary, as soon as my father left me off and our Subaru Outback disappeared down the road, Ryon and Carlos descended upon me. I can't remember what they said, but I know that it hurt my feelings. Every single day that school year they were mean to me.

I never told my father. When he asked, "How's it going?"

I said, "good." I was afraid he'd home-school me again before I made any friends.

But it wasn't easy to make friends. Nobody was very friendly to me. I don't know if they didn't like me, or if they were too scared to be nice because of Ryon and Carlos.

Third grade was worse. More kids picked on me. I didn't want to go to school anymore. I pretended I was sick. My father let me stay home for a few days, but then he caught on that I wasn't really sick. I told him it was too hard for me to wear my leg brace so much. He took me to see Doctor Martin who said that there was no reason why I couldn't wear the brace all day long every day at school.

That night at dinner Dad said, "If you want to go to school, Avery, you're going to have to not let your brace bother you."

"But I don't want to go to school," I blurted out.

"Why?" he asked.

I panicked. For some reason I couldn't tell him the truth. I searched my brain for an answer. "Because the work is too hard," I lied.

"Your grades are good Avery," he said as he piled up our dirty dinner plates and silverware.

"I was too easy on you. Now you're just lazy." He took the dishes into the kitchen and opened the dishwasher. He came back to get the glasses. "You can't let a little hard work bother you either," he said, then returned to the kitchen and turned on the hot water at the sink.

I put my head on the dining room table and shut my eyes. I thought, *Whenever I'm upset about anything, Dad always says, "Don't let it bother you." If I told him about the kids being mean to me he'd probably just tell me to not let it bother me.*

But it did bother me. A lot.

Avery Quinn: *Rescue*

After lunch the seventh day of fourth grade, our class met the new gym teacher. He had dark hair and eyes and looked like a tall, thin version of Enzo.

"My name is Mr. Sergiovanti," he told us. "You can call me Mr. Sergio."

I always hated gym class, but not that day. We played a kick-ball game where you kept one foot glued to the floor and kicked the ball with your other foot. For the first time I competed as well as my classmates did.

Every year my father got a letter from the school that said, because I was disabled, I could have extra physical education time with the gym teacher. I never wanted to do it and Dad said I didn't have to. But this teacher was better than the old one. I hoped it wasn't too late to sign up.

There were so many piles of papers in my Dad's bedroom that it took him a long time to find the letter. "Is this what you're looking for?" he asked me one night.

The letter stated that Mr. Sergiovanti was a Physical Education teacher, a Social Skills instructor, and an Adaptive Physical Education facilitator for children with disabilities. There were two boxes to check. One was marked Adaptive Physical Education and the other Social Skills Instruction. Dad checked both boxes.

Two weeks later, when the kids in my class lined up for recess, I stood at the back of the line, clutching my hall pass. They went outside. I headed for the gym. My extra Phys Ed time was about to begin.

I found Mr. Sergio in his office juggling three rainbow colored Koosh balls. He smiled, put down the balls and shook my right hand. "We're going to have a great time, Avery," he said.

I was happy to be where I wouldn't be picked on.

"Let's start with stretches. These are good for your left hand and arm."

Mr. Sergio curled the fingers of his left hand a little and lightly tapped them up and down his right arm. I took my left hand out of my pocket and did the same.

"My Dad isn't interested in sports," I told him.

"How about you?"

"I haven't had much practice."

"Well, here's your chance," he said.

Several days later we were doing what Mr. Sergio called our warm-up exercises. He held his arms out straight and moved his hands in little circles, first one direction and then the other. I followed what he did.

"Don't forget to breathe," he said, taking in a deep breath and slowly letting it out.

I did the same. Mr. Sergio raised his fingers to his shoulders, brought them down, and raised them again. I copied him.

"I see that some kids are bullying you," he said.

My arms dropped to my side.

"I had the same kind of problem when I was your age."

I gaped at him.

"My grandfather talked with the school principal and he also taught me what he called his bully blocking techniques."

"I wish someone would block out these guys," I blurted out.

Mr. Sergio picked up a yellow beanbag from a box by his desk. He looked up and threw the beanbag high above his head. "Bully blocking is not about fighting or getting back at kids who are mean," he said, catching the beanbag on its way down. "It's about using your brain," he pointed to his head, "and keeping your cool." He tossed the beanbag to me. "I can show you how."

"I don't think so," I said, clumsily catching the beanbag with my right hand.

"Why not?"

"It's kind of hopeless," I said, tossing the bag back. "You're not going to tell my father are you?"

"You don't want him to know?"

"I think I should tell him myself," I said, catching the beanbag with both hands.

"Sure," said Mr. Sergio. "Anybody been helping you?"

I was embarrassed to answer. "No," I said.

We threw the beanbag back and forth. The more we did, the easier it was to catch.

"Your father can talk to our principal. In the meantime I think I can help you develop some confidence," said Mr. Sergio.

I shrugged my shoulders.

"That's a good exercise," said Mr. Sergio. "Leave your arms down and raise your shoulders as high as you can. Then let them drop. Do it three times."

I did what he told me to do.

Shrugging your shoulders is also a good thing to do when a kid says something you don't like. Instead of looking scared you could shrug your shoulders and look like you don't care what they say. He put the beanbag down, picked up a white Whiffle ball, and handed it to me.

"How many times can you catch this before it drops?" he asked.

I tossed the ball in the air and caught it twenty-five times before I missed.

"What are they saying to you?"

I told him what I could remember.

"The school staff aren't helping?"

"I don't think they know."

"It's been hard, huh?"

I nodded and then regretted it because my eyes started to water and burn.

"You are getting verbally harassed, Avery. There are plenty of things you can do or say that might just get them to stop."

No, I thought, and turned away so he couldn't see my face. *I can't stop these guys. Why don't you do it? Don't leave it up to me.*

"You haven't been responding to the kids who bully you. That's good. It's actually one of my grandfather's bully blocking skills. But when you don't respond you need to look confident, as if saying nothing is your choice, not because you're too frightened to say something. Speaking up is another choice. How about pretending to be your tormentors and say the things they say to you?"

"Tormentors?" I asked, looking at him sideways.

"Torment: to annoy, harass, tease. Tormentors, the kids who pick on you," said Mr. Sergio.

I put the Whiffle ball back on his desk.

"Want to give it a try?"

I was silent.

"What do you have to lose?"

I wasn't sure what to say.

"Let me show you," he said.

"Whatever," I replied.

"Tell me something they said to you this morning?" he asked.

"Pirate, where's your hook?" I said.

"Try that again with a meaner tone of voice," instructed Mr. Sergio.

It was easier to do than I thought it would be.

"Leave me alone," answered Mr. Sergio.

I put my hand over my mouth to hide my smile.

"Give me another."

"What's wrong with you?" I said, pretending to be Carlos.

"Stop bothering me," answered Mr. Sergio.

"Run any marathons?"

"Quit it," Mr. Sergio said in a tough-sounding voice.

I figured it would be a million years before I could sound like that. I didn't expect to like acting like the kids who were bothering me, but I did. After a while Mr. Sergio and I switched places. I practiced saying the things Mr. Sergio had taught me while Mr. Sergio pretended to be mean.

"Get away from kids who treat you with disrespect as soon as you can. I know that's kind of hard to do at the beginning of the school day and when you can't walk that fast."

I nodded.

"You could at least stop drooping your shoulders and looking down."

I didn't understand what he was talking about.

What would it feel like to hold your back straight and your head high? Even if you don't feel confident, you can try to look as if you do."

I didn't answer.

"There are three ways we can act: passive, aggressive, and assertive. This is what passive looks like."

Mr. Sergio walked away from me with his back bent over, looking at the ground.

I thought, *I guess that's what I look like.*

He quickly turned around and said, "Now for aggressive."

He ran up to a gym wall, slammed his hands against it, and yelled, "Stupid blockhead. No, you get out of *my* way."

I laughed.

Mr. Sergio walked towards me looking his usual tall, friendly self. "This is an assertive way to walk. Assertive is the best."

I nodded.

"Now you try it."

I took a few steps, slumped over and looked at the floor. I was used to doing that.

"Passive," said Mr. Sergio snapping his fingers.

I walked up to a wall, slapped my right hand on it and said, "Blockhead, get out of my way."

"Aggressive," said Mr. Sergio, snapping his fingers again.

I straightened my shoulders, held my head high, looked Mr. Sergio in the eye and walked toward him.

"Assertive," he shouted, pointing his thumbs upward. "Excellent! He rubbed his hands together. "Now repeat after me. Quit it."

"Quit it," I said.

"Stop."

"Stop," I said.

"Leave me alone."

"Leave me alone."

"Stop bothering me."

"Stop bothering me."

"Cut it out."

"What's wrong with me?" I asked. "How come nobody likes me?"

"It is not your fault you're being bullied. Something has happened in these kids lives that causes them to act the way they do. I bet you'll be popular some day, once people get to know you."

I shrugged my shoulders.

"So, what are *you* interested in?"

He rolled one of the Whiffle balls across the floor.

"Earth Science," I said, kicking the ball back. "Natural disasters."

"Learned anything interesting?"

He passed me the Whiffle ball using the inside of his foot.

"If the heat released by an average hurricane in one day could be converted to electricity, it would supply the United States' electrical needs for about six months."

I kicked the ball with the instep of my right foot.

"Really? What else?"

"A tropical storm becomes a hurricane when wind speed reaches seventy-five miles per hour."

"And?"

"Hurricanes are hundreds of miles wide. They last for days or weeks. In India people call them cyclones. The Chinese call them typhoons, and in Australia they are called willy-willies."

"Try it with your other foot," said Mr. Sergio, kicking the ball with his left foot. "Tell me more."

"The first hurricane of every year gets a name that begins with A. The next name begins with B, then C, until the end of the alphabet. But some letters are never used."

"Which ones?"

"Q, U, X, Y, and Z."

"I remember hurricanes named Andrew, Betsy, Dean, Felix, Hugo, Humberto, Katrina and Rita," said Mr. Sergio.

"If a hurricane gets a girl's name, then the next one is named after a boy," I said.

"Would you like to be a Meteorologist someday?"

"I want to be a hurricane hunter pilot."

"What's that?"

28

"Pilots who fly planes into the eye of a hurricane to get information that can help save people's lives."

"Never heard of it," said Mr. Sergio. "How about you teach me about natural disasters while I teach you about bully blocking?"

"I guess," I said thinking *bully blocking was fine for his grandfather and him, but not me. Mr. Sergio is an athlete. That's like the total opposite from me.*

"Try again," he said. He picked up the Whiffle ball and handed it to me again. "How many times can you catch it?" He counted aloud. "Twenty-six," he said when I dropped the ball. "If you want to change your behavior from passive to assertive, that's how you do it, little by little by little."

I nodded, saying to myself, *who said I want to change my behavior? What good would that do?*

"All this talk about earth science reminds me of quicksand," said Mr. Sergio. "When people fall into quicksand they usually panic, struggle, and get stuck. But if they were to breathe deeply and move slowly, they could get into a float position on their backs, and paddle themselves to solid ground. Getting bullied is like being in quicksand. The more you panic the worse things get. If you stay calm however, you can get yourself free."

I pictured Ryon, Carlos, and Enzo chasing me in a jungle and pushing me into a pool of quicksand. *Yeah sure,* I thought, *I breathe d-e-e-p-l-y, move s-l-o-w-l-y, float around some, and paddle back to shore. Then they push me in again and the quicksand gobbles me up. Who is this guy kidding?*

Chapter Discussion

Discuss *Avery Quinn: Rumblings* and *Avery Quinn: Rescue.* Ask students to refrain from using children's real names when discussing disrespect and bullying. Advise them to communicate with you privately later if they need to.

Create a chart for the class to see, with the numbers 1–5 in a vertical line corresponding with two columns, one titled Agree and the other Disagree. After each question, record on the chart the number of hands raised. It is not necessary to require every student to vote. Some will have opinions and others may not.

1. Raise your hand if you agree with Mr. Sergio that it is better to be assertive than passive or aggressive. Raise your hand if you disagree with Mr. Sergio's statement. Why do you agree or disagree?

2. 80% of 250 young people surveyed reported that they liked to tease to make someone miserable. Raise your hand if you think that this is true at our school. Raise your hand if you think this is not true at our school. Why do you agree or disagree?

3. There is bullying happening at our school. Raise your hand if you agree. Raise your hand if you disagree. For those that agree, how many think that teachers and the principal know about it? How many think that teachers and the principal do not know about it?

4. *It is dangerous to respond to bullying with aggression.* Raise your hand if you agree. Raise your hand if you disagree. Why do you agree or disagree?

5. *If a student acts in an annoying way (s)he deserves to be treated with disrespect.* Raise your hand if you agree. Raise your hand if you disagree. Why do you agree or disagree?

SPEAK UP FOR YOURSELF #1

This activity requires at least two people: one to read the disrespectful statements and the other to be Avery speaking up for himself.

When you pretend to be Avery, stand tall, pull your shoulders back, hold your head high, and speak in a calm voice without yelling.

Disrespectful Statements	**Assertive Responses**
Pirate, where's your hook?	Leave me alone.
What's wrong with you?	Stop making fun of me.
Avery is a girl.	Quit it.
If it isn't the sportsman Avery Quinn.	Cut it out.
Are you deaf or just dumb?	No

After completing this assignment, de-brief. Call each other by your real names and ask each other...

- What did it feel like to read the disrespectful statements?
- What did it feel like to read the assertive statements?

SPEAK UP FOR YOURSELF #2

1. Repeat the *Speak Up For Yourself #1* activity with a family member, friend, neighbor, or teacher. When you are done, de-brief by asking your partner how it felt to read the disrespectful and assertive statements. Record their answers.

    a. How did it feel to read the disrespectful statements?

_____

_____

_____

_____

_____

    b. How did it feel to read the assertive statements?

_____

_____

_____

_____

_____

2. Circle the correct description of your partner.

    Family member: mother   father   sister   brother   grandparent   aunt   uncle   other

                     friend   neighbor   teacher

RESPECT & DISRESPECT

1. Put #1 next to each of the following examples that show how people in our school treat each other with respect.

Respectful Actions

____ Ask permission

____ Listen

____ Cooperate

____ Compromise

____ Collaborate

____ Problem-solve

____ Pay attention

____ Encourage

____ Tell the truth

____ Say how they feel

____ Share

____ Ask for help

____ Be friendly

____ Wave hello and goodbye

____ Give high-fives

____ Give thumbs-up

____ Make something for someone

____ Hold a door open

____ Smile

____ Help

____ Ask someone to do something fun with them

____ Say something nice about someone

____ Use positive words: Good Morning. Thank you. Please.

____ Give compliments: Nice job. Good idea. Awesome.

____ Talk it over

____ Offer to help

____ Speak op for yourself

____ Speak up for others

____ Build

____ Do schoolwork and homework

____ Wait your turn

____ Follow directions

____ Teamwork

____ Volunteer

____ Raise hand

2. Put #2 next to each of the following examples that show how people in our school treat each other with disrespect.

Disrespectful Actions

Physical

____ Hit	____ Punch	____ Grab, steal or destroy
____ Trip	____ Step on	belongings
____ Kick	____ Scratch	____ Inflict or attempt
____ Bite	____ Pull hair	to inflict injury or
____ Push	____ Uninvited touch	discomfort
____ Slap	____ Throw objects at	____ Force someone to do
____ Shove	____ Get in someone's face	something they don't
____ Choke	____ Wrestle to the ground	want to do
____ Pinch	____ Pull someone's clothes off	

Verbal

____ Insult	____ Call names	____ Tell someone they stink
____ Gossip	____ Be sarcastic	____ Maliciously tease and taunt
____ Pick on	____ Demand money	____ Repeat what someone
____ Swear at	____ Say something mean	says in a mocking way
____ Threaten	____ Make harassing phone	____ Convince someone's
____ Be bossy	calls	friend to stop
____ Put-down	____ Spread lies and rumors	liking him or her

Non-verbal

____ Dirty looks	____ Give someone the *silent*	____ Hold one's nose when
____ Point and laugh at	*treatment*	someone walks by
____ Create a hate club	____ Treat someone as if they	____ Send a mean note, e-mail,
____ Use obscene gestures	are invisible	or instant or text message
____ Spread rumors on the	____ Exclude from games and	
Internet	other activities	

3. What examples are missing from the *Respectful Actions* chart?

_____

_____

_____

_____

4. What examples are missing from the *Disrespectful Actions* chart?

_____

_____

_____

_____

5. Put #5 next to any actions listed on the *Respectful Actions* and *Disrespectful Actions* charts that are sometimes respectful and sometimes disrespectful.

Discussion: Respect & Disrespect

Discuss the students' responses to the Handout: *Respect & Disrespect*. Ask them not to use children's real names during this conversation. Advise them to communicate with you privately later if they need to.

1. How do people at our school treat each other with
   a. respect?
   b. disrespect?

2. What respectful actions would you add to the *Respectful Actions* chart to make it more complete?

3. What disrespectful actions would you add to the *Disrespectful Actions* chart to make it more complete?

4. Which actions could be both respectful and disrespectful?

5. What happens more often at our school, respect or disrespect?

Practice Observation

1. Create a chart like the one below for the class to see.

2. Ask students to describe ten actions they have seen or heard happen at your school. (Again without using anyone's real names.)

3. For each action have students identify whether the action is an example of respect or disrespect. Put an R next to respectful actions and a D next to disrespectful actions. Put R/D next to those that could be both.

Actions	**Respectful (R) or Disrespectful (D)**
1. _____	_____
2. _____	_____
3. _____	_____
4. _____	_____
5. _____	_____
6. _____	_____
7. _____	_____
8. _____	_____
9. _____	_____
10. _____	_____

ONE-DAY OBSERVATION

1. For one school day observe other people's behavior. Record five actions you see or hear. Do not record anyone's real name.

2. For each action note the time of day.

3. Put an R next to respectful actions and a D next to disrespectful actions.

Actions	Respectful or Disrespectful	Time
1. _____	_____	_____
2. _____	_____	_____
3. _____	_____	_____
4. _____	_____	_____
5. _____	_____	_____

Empowering Children to Help Stop Bullying at School

TWO-DAY OBSERVATION

1. For two days observe other people's behavior. Record five actions you see or hear. Do not record anyone's real name.

2. For each action note the date and time of day.

3. Put an R next to respectful actions and a D next to disrespectful actions.

Actions	Respectful or Disrespectful	Date	Time
1. _____	_____	_____	_____
2. _____	_____	_____	_____
3. _____	_____	_____	_____
4. _____	_____	_____	_____
5. _____	_____	_____	_____

HANDOUT

NATEL

Courage in My Life

I think courage is being brave and standing up for yourself. Such as, choosing the right friends, and recognizing what friendship really is.

One day in third grade, there used to be this group of girls who I thought were cool. I tried so hard to fit in with them. I tried to act like them; I even tried to dress like them. I was really desperate to be in their group.

Soon the girls said I could be in their group. I was so excited. I ran home and shared my amazing day with my mom. The next day, I tried to talk to my new friends, but they ignored me. I didn't understand why my new friends were acting that way. I felt hurt and betrayed. I was so confused. That day, I ran home feeling angry and sad at the same time. My mom wondered what was wrong. I didn't want to tell her how I felt and what happened.

The next day I went to school. I was angrier than ever. The girls wanted to talk to me, but I didn't want to talk to them. I told them that I didn't want to be friends with them anymore. They were so surprised because no one had ever stood up to them before. I think I had a lot of courage to walk away from something that I thought I wanted to be a part of. I also realized what real friendship is and it is not about being in a cool group.

The Courage of Boston's Children, Volume XVI, The Max Warburg Courage Curriculum, Inc. and the Boston Public Schools, Houghton Mifflin Company, 2007.

1. Why did Natel want to be in the "cool" group?

2. Why didn't Natel want to tell her Mom about the new "friends" not speaking to her?

3. How did Natel stand up for herself?

4. What do Natel and Avery have in common?

5. How are Natel and Avery different?

MICHAEL

Courage in My Life

Courage is when you stick up for someone or for yourself, and don't let anyone tell you what to do. An act of courage for me was when I was bullied in the third grade by a fourth grader; we'll call him by the nickname, Muscle Head. Muscle Head was the biggest, most ruthless, strongest kid in the fourth grade that I had ever known.

Every time I tried to tell the teacher that he was picking on me, I would hear little whispers that I was a snitch or a tattletale, when I knew I wasn't. One day Muscle Head called me a name that I will never forget! So at recess I finally snapped and decided to stand up for myself. I told him to stop making fun of me. After that day Muscle Head never bullied me again, and I have lived in peace and harmony.

The lesson of this story is that there will always be someone who will bully you or will want to start trouble with you, but you have to have the courage and confidence to stand up for yourself. Be sure to tell somebody about your problem no matter what anyone says.

The Courage of Boston's Children, Volume XVII, The Max Warburg Courage Curriculum, Inc. and the Boston Public Schools, Northeastern University, 2008.

1. What were the words Michael used to stick up for himself?

_____

2. Why do you think "Muscle Head" never bullied Michael again.

_____

_____

3. What do Michael and Avery have in common?

_____

_____

4. How are Michael and Avery different?

_____

_____

5. Do you agree with Michael *"that there will always be someone who will bully you or will want to start trouble with you"*? Explain your answer.

_____

_____

6. Do you agree with Michael when he says, *"Be sure to tell somebody about your problem no matter what anyone says"*? Explain your answer.

_____

_____

ZHONGMEI

...I don't know who my birth parents are. That is because I am adopted from China. Ever since kindergarten, kids have been curious about why I don't look like either of my parents. They ask mean questions like, "Why didn't your parents want you anymore?" "Did your parents throw you away?" "So who are your real parents?" At this point, usually I feel like crying. I feel like screaming, "I don't know, okay?! I just don't know!" This is the question that makes me feel the most frustrated: "So how come your parents sold you? Is it because they did not have enough money?"

*The Courage of Boston's Children,*Volume XV, The Max Warburg Courage Curriculum, Inc. and the Boston Public Schools, Houghton Mifflin Company, 2006.

1. Do you agree that the following questions are "mean"? Write yes or no after each question.

   a. "Why didn't your parents want you anymore?" _____

   b. Did your parents throw you away? _____

   c. "So who are your real parents?" _____

   d. "So how come your parents sold you? Is it because they did not have enough money?" _____

2. What do Zhongmei and Avery have in common?

_____

_____

3. How are Zhongmei and Avery different?

_____

_____

_____

4. What can Zhongmei do to help solve her problem?

_____

_____

_____

THREE

Who Bullies?

Objectives

• To provide students with illustrations of ways they can respectfully stick up for themselves when treated with disrespect.

• To explore the concept of bullying.

• To identify characteristics of bullying leaders and followers.

• To introduce the concept of Respect Agreements.

• To help students develop assertive communication skills.

• To explore ways students can help stop bullying at school.

Chapter Summary, *Avery Quinn: Warming Up*

After many weeks of practice, Avery starts to assert himself. The bullying however continues. Avery does become more confident and experiences a little success.

Suggestions for Success

1. Mr. Sergio in *Avery Quinn* does not inform other school staff or directly intervene with the students who bully Avery. The text was written this way so that a range of strategies to deal with verbal harassment could be shown. If you know of a child in your school who is bullied, it is recommended that you work with other staff to:
   a. provide the child with support,
   b. curtail the freedom of those who bully,
   c. provide consistent consequences in a calm manner, and
   d. continue to treat all students with respect.

2. Assertiveness skills help students respond to mild forms of bullying. Children like Avery, who experience more serious types of bullying, should not be expected to stop the bullying themselves. Adults need to support these children rather than expect them to change.

3. Instead of advice, provide students with empathy and help them brainstorm options.

4. The following conditions at home may cause a child to develop bullying behaviors.
   • a lack of warmth and emotional nurturing
   • permissiveness, with a lack of limits set on children's behavior
   • at times, harsh discipline with verbally aggressive outbursts by adults

   It is important that schools do not replicate what a child who bullies may have experienced at home. The recommended model for schools to follow is to increase supervision in targeted areas and use caring consequences for disrespectful behavior while maintaining a nurturing relationship with all students, including those who bully.

Activities

Avery Quinn: Warming Up.

   a. Read aloud *Avery Quinn: Warming Up*.

   b. Use the Chapter Discussion questions to stimulate a class
      conversation about the chapter.

Select from the recommended activities below, especially those in bold.

1. Role-plays: Speak Up for Yourself #3

   Involve either small groups or the whole class in role-plays. Use
   approach a or b.

   a. Divide students into pairs. Give each child the Handout: *Speak
      Up for Yourself #3*.

      • Explain that one student will read the disrespectful statements
        and the other will pretend to be Avery speaking up for himself.
        Everyone speaking as Avery should stand tall, pull their
        shoulders back, hold their head high, and talk calmly without
        yelling.

      • After students have done the role-play once, they switch places.
        The one who played Avery first now reads the disrespectful
        statement and vice versa.

      • When students are done, they de-brief by calling each other
        their real names and asking how it felt to read the disrespectful
        and assertive statements.

   b. If the group needs more structure, the teacher can read the
      disrespectful statements and one at a time, or the whole group
      together, give the assertive responses.

      • At the end of the activity, de-brief by calling students by their
        real names. Ask them how it felt to give the assertive responses.

      • Instruct children to save the Handout: *Speak Up for Yourself #3*
        to use with their homework assignment.

2. Homework: Speak Up for Yourself #4

   a. Distribute the Handout: *Speak Up for Yourself #4* to each student.

   b. Children repeat the *Speak Up for Yourself #3* activity with a family
      member, friend, neighbor, or teacher and turn in their completed
      Speak Up for Yourself #4 handouts.

3. Homework: Interview—Speak Up for Yourself

   a. Give each student the Handout: *Interview—Speak Up for Yourself.*
      Also give them a copy of the Handout: *Respect & Disrespect* or the
      Master *Disrespect Chart* you created in section Two.

   b. Children interview a family member, friend, neighbor, or
      teacher about a time he or she were treated with disrespect and
      were afraid to stand up for him/herself. Interview responses are
      recorded on the Handout: *Interview—Speak Up for Yourself.*

c. As a class, children verbally share their interview data and compare and contrast responses. Afterwards they turn in their completed handouts.

4. Danny: a victim of bullying
   a. Read aloud Danny's essay.
   b. Talk about how speaking up is not the only way to deal with disrespect and might not always be the best choice. Sometimes it is too dangerous to speak up to children who bully and much more important to ask adults for help.

5. Who Bullies?
   a. Distribute the Handout: *Who Bullies?* for students to read and complete.
   b. Use the *Discussion: Who Bullies?* questions as guides to stimulate a class conversation about who bullies. Afterwards students turn in their completed work.

6. Homework: Leaders of Bullying
   a. Distribute the Handout: *Leaders of Bullying* for children to complete individually and turn in.

7. Respect Agreements
   Divide students into pairs or small groups, or do this activity with the whole class.
   a. Give each pair or group a copy of the Handout: *Respect & Disrespect* (or the Master copy you made in section Two) and the Handout: *Respect Agreement.* When doing this activity with the whole class you will need only one *Respect Agreement.*
   b. In pairs, groups, or as a class, students discuss and list the respectful ways they want to be treated by peers at school.
   c. Each pair, group, or the whole class agrees on three ways they will try to treat each other with respect.
   d. Each pair, group member, or class member signs the *Respect Agreement* that they helped create.
   e. Collect the agreements to use later with the *Respect Agreement Meeting* activity in section Five.

8. **Journal**
   Students respond to the following assignment in their journals.
   a. Describe a bullying leader.
   b. Describe a bullying follower.
   c. If you went to Parker Elementary School and saw Avery bullied, what do you think you would do? Explain your answer.
   d. Speaking up for yourself can be a very difficult thing to do. Explain why.

Avery Quinn: *Warming Up*

I spent recess every day in the gym. I liked exercising more than wandering around the playground trying to avoid Ryon, Carlos and Enzo. To make Mr. Sergio happy I let him teach me how to be assertive. I got good at walking tall with my shoulders back and my head high. It was too hard for me to speak up for real, but I knew what I *wanted* to say.

When Enzo asked me, "Why aren't you at recess?" I looked away, but in my head I shouted, *"Shut up!"*

Ryon asked, "Hiding in the nurse's office, sickie?" I bit my tongue so I wouldn't say, *"Talk to me again and I'll punch you in the mouth."*

When Carlos exclaimed, "We miss you s-o much!" I covered my ears so I wouldn't scream, *"Like you care."*

Mr. Sergio seemed to guess my thoughts. "Doing or saying the first angry thing that comes into your head keeps you stuck in bullying quicksand," he said. "Sometimes it's hard to tell the difference between aggressive and assertive. The key is to slow down and take a breath before you speak. Then you can float and paddle yourself to shore."

I imagined I was floating on a raft, paddling around in the Nashua River. I thought, *if only I didn't have to go to school.*

That night I lay awake staring at the silhouette of a paper mache volcano I made for a second grade science project. I was worrying about what was going to happen to me. Through the screen of my bedroom window, I heard the sad whistle of a whip-poor-will. *Will I always be lonely?* I wondered. *If only I could hide from everyone like the whip-poor-will does.* My Dad taught me that some people think whip-poor-wills are omens of bad luck. *Things are going to get worse.* I convinced myself. *I know it.*

I remembered a poem my father made me memorize when I was seven: *Hear the lonesome whip-*

poor-will. He sounds too blue to fly. The midnight train is whining low. I'm so lonesome, I could cry. I wondered, *would Dad like that song so much if Mom was still alive?*

In the morning I told my father about having heard a whip-poor-will.

"Whip-poor-wills are usually gone by now but with this extraordinarily hot weather we're having, everything's thrown off. Did I tell you that Whip-poor-will's nests are on the ground?"

"Why?" I asked.

"I don't know," he said. "The female lays two eggs at a time and will stay on her nest unless almost stepped on."

"That's stupid," I said.

"Sometimes they get eaten by dogs," Dad said.

I'm like a Whip-poor-will, I thought, *just waiting to get stepped on or eaten up.*

Weeks went by. One afternoon I was walking down the driveway to our cabin, distracted by the memory of Ryon's cruel words, when a hawk flew past only a few feet away. I saw its dark eye, the circular hole on its hooked beak, and its red tail. Chasing the hawk was an eastern kingbird. The wingspan of the hawk was four times the size of the kingbird's. Yet the tiny black, white and gray bird chased the hawk past the tops of the tree's multi-colored leaves, far into the sky until I couldn't see them anymore.

Something clicked in my head. I cupped my hands to my mouth and called out loud to the brave kingbird, "I'll do it Wednesday."

Wednesday turned out to be gray and rainy. I tried not to step in mud puddles on my walk down our driveway but wasn't successful. My shoes were drenched. I shivered in the front seat of the bus and wished I wasn't so alone.

"Wavery, are you crying?" I heard Ryon ask. He sounded like he was close by.

I watched the windshield wipers go back and forth.

"I hope I didn't hurt your feelings," he said.

My blood was boiling. I imagined steam spewing from the top of my head.

"Cry baby. Wavery wet himself," Ryon continued.

I took a deep breath and thought, *do it*. I turned around.

Ryon was two rows back across the aisle. He was wearing a black and white soccer shirt.

"Are you giving me the evil eye?" he laughed, though his face looked angry.

"No."

"You said something," Ryon exclaimed. "I can't believe it. You said a word."

I swallowed hard. "Stop it," I said.

"Two words, a sentence," mocked Ryon. "A two-year-old can do that."

I turned away.

"You want me to stop Wavery? But I can't."

I had said something. Spoken up. I wondered, *What am I supposed to do next?*

Ryon went on and on about how I was in pre-school just learning the alphabet and all. I kept my head up by fixing my eyes on the blur of rain beating against the window, the big wipers pushing it this way and that.

By the time we arrived at school the sun was shining. A faint rainbow hung in the sky. Kids were playing soccer in front of the school, despite the sogginess of the field. Ryon ran right past me to join them. *Things will get better now*, I thought, *Ryon likes soccer more than bugging me*. I got all the way to the front doors before Carlos, Enzo, and Marcella crossed my path.

Carlos, as usual, was surrounded by fifth grade girls. "Hey, knock knees," he taunted.

My knees were shaking. I wanted to say, "knock it off." I limped as fast as I could to my classroom. Enzo was next to me, bending and shaking his knees. Copycat Marcella tried to do the same.

"Mr. Knock Knees," sang Enzo.

"Knock knock joke knees," said Marcella.

My hands felt cold and sweaty. *I can do this*, I told myself. In a voice that was too quiet and quivery, I said, "My name is Avery."

"Oh really," mocked Enzo.

Our teachers called us to come into our classrooms. Marcella was yelled at for not being with the third graders where she belonged. It took all morning for me to calm myself. I didn't hear a word that my teacher said.

"Congratulations," said Mr. Sergio at recess, making a motion with his arms that looked like he had a bat in his hands and was hitting a baseball into the air. "Your hard work is paying off."

I wasn't sure. That afternoon and the next morning, I was too scared to speak up to Ryon and Carlos, but determined to stand up to the other two. Enzo and Marcella, on each side of me, pretended to limp.

"Slow poke has spoke," teased Enzo.

"Slowpoke spoke," repeated Marcella in her high-pitched whiney voice.

I stopped and looked Enzo in the eye. In a voice that was louder than I usually spoke I said, "leave me alone," and walked into class.

"Wow," I heard someone say.

Chapter Discussion

Discuss *Avery Quinn: Warming Up*. Ask students not to use children's real names during this conversation. Advise them to communicate privately later if they need to.

1. How is Avery treated disrespectfully?
2. How does he respond?
3. How is he feeling?
4. What might happen next?
5. When Avery tried to deal with the bullying by himself, how successful was he?
6. What changed when Mr. Sergio helped him?

INTERVIEW—
SPEAK UP FOR YOURSELF

A. Choose a family member, friend, neighbor, or teacher to interview. Show him/her the *Respect & Disrespect* handout.

    1. Ask the person to tell you about a time when they were treated with disrespect and were afraid to speak up.

    2. Record their answer.

_____

_____

_____

_____

_____

_____

_____

_____

_____

_____

_____

B. Circle the correct description of your partner.

Family member: mother   father   sister   brother   grandparent   aunt   uncle   other

                      friend   neighbor   teacher

SPEAK UP FOR YOURSELF #3

This activity requires at least two people: one to read the disrespectful statements and the other to pretend to be Avery speaking up for himself.

When you pretend to be Avery stand tall, pull your shoulders back, hold your head high, take a breath and speak in a calm voice without yelling.

Disrespectful Statements	Assertive Responses
Cry baby.	Stop annoying me.
Knock-knees.	Knock it off.
Mr. Knock-Knees.	My name is Avery.
Knock knock joke knees.	I don't like that.
Slow poke.	Please stop.
Hiding in the nurse's office, sickie?	Maybe, maybe not.
(Point at your partner and pretend to laugh. Ha. Ha. Ha.)	Don't laugh at me.

After completing this assignment, de-brief. Call each other by your real names. Ask...

• What did it feel like to read the disrespectful statements?
• What did it feel like to read the assertive statements?

SPEAK UP FOR YOURSELF #4

Repeat the *Speak Up for Yourself #3* activity with a family member, friend, neighbor, or teacher. When you are done, de-brief. Ask your partner how it felt for him or her to read the disrespectful and respectful statements. Record his or her answers.

1. How did it feel to read the disrespectful statements?

_____

_____

_____

_____

2. How did it feel to read the respectful statements?

_____

_____

_____

_____

3. Circle the correct description of your partner.

Family member: mother   father   sister   brother   grandparent   aunt   uncle   other

friend   neighbor   teacher

DANNY

Courage in My Life

To me, courage means being strong in mind and having the power to stand up for your rights. That's just what I did. My ethnicity is Asian so people make fun of me. That is, until I had had enough.

Ever since I was in kindergarten people have made fun of me by saying things in what they thought was my native language. They always picked on me and called me names like "yellow belly" or "teacher's pet." Once in kindergarten they even shoved me into a closet during recess and left me there for half an hour. I was taught that fighting and doing bad was a sin and that I shouldn't yell or fight back. I also didn't know how to defend myself then. It was all wrong. I then learned that it was not wrong to fight back if I had to protect myself.

Every time someone called me a name I just asked them, "How would you feel if I called you _____?" That stopped them from calling me names but it also brought more trouble. A lot of kids would try to jump me at almost every corner. I managed to escape every time except for once when I got cornered and got beat up pretty bad. I panicked and called the police and the kids stopped trying to jump me. Still, every so often I still think that the kids have a grudge against me.

The Courage of Boston's Children,Volume XV, The Max Warburg Courage Curriculum, Inc. and the Boston Public Schools, Houghton Mifflin Company, 2006.

WHO BULLIES?

I admit it. I was a bully. You name it I've done it. I've called kids names, made fun of kids' weight, made kids cry of embarrassment and many other terrible things you can imagine. Ever since the first grade, I've always been the tallest kid in the class. I used that size as an advantage. I hung out with all the troublemakers in the class, just trying to fit in.

During all of this I never took into consideration that I was hurting someone else's feelings. I was with the "cool kids" and that was all that mattered to me. Each day the gang and I would randomly select our new victim.

This one kid that comes to mind is "Will." Will was a little overweight and was not popular. He was smart, always did his homework, and never bothered anybody. This was Will's unlucky week in the third grade. I continued to do this for a long time. Taunting and teasing this "good kid" was becoming an everyday occurrence. This whole time I was hurting Will's feelings more and more each day, never thinking about how he felt or how it may affect him.

Reprinted from an essay Thomas wrote that was published in *The Courage of Boston's Children*, Volume XIV, Houghton Mifflin Company, 2005.

Children who bully can be male or female, rich or poor, on the honor role or getting bad grades, living in the country or the city, and preschoolers or teenagers. Males at school who bully usually use disrespectful actions that are direct like teasing, hitting, and calling people names. Females at school who bully usually use disrespectful actions that are indirect like gossip, rumors, lies, dirty looks, talking behind someone's back, and excluding a girl from a group or activity.

In the 1980's Dan Olweus, a professor of psychology in Norway was curious about bullying. His research on the subject was the first large-scale scientific study of bullying that had ever been done in the world. Mr. Olweus and his team of researchers discovered that there are children who lead the bullying and those who follow. Since the 1980's many researchers have found similar results.

It seems that many children who are leaders of bullying have early childhood experiences that effect their personalities and behavior. Depending on how little love, supervision, and kind discipline the child experienced in his or her family, the student may end up with a habit of looking for children who are not assertive and treating them disrespectfully over and over again.

Leaders of bullying often have several other characteristics. They may:

- be bossy,
- have a short temper,
- refuse to follow rules, and
- be more popular and confident than those they bully.

Their choice of behavior style is aggressive.

If they are boys, they may be physically stronger than those they are mean to.

If they are girls, they may be more attractive than those they are mean to.

Other children become bullies by following and joining in with the bullying leaders. It is hard for leaders of bullying to change when other children support what they are doing.

In the story *Avery Quinn*, Ryon and Carlos are bullying leaders. Enzo, Marcella, and students who laugh when Avery is treated with disrespect are followers.

Children who join in on the bullying that someone else starts often have several of the following characteristics. They may:

- think bullying is fun,
- admire the leaders of bullying,
- not feel responsible for their behavior,
- lack confidence and assertiveness skills,
- think they won't get in trouble for being disrespectful,
- think that bullying leaders become popular by acting mean,
- think that joining in on bullying will make themselves more popular, and/or
- believe that those who are bullied deserve to be treated with disrespect.

1. Choose a character from a book, TV show, movie, or video game who is an example of a bullying leader or follower.

   a. Name of the character _____

   b. Name of the book, TV show, movie or video game_____

   _____

c. Describe the character's behavior.

   _____

   _____

   _____

   _____

2. Check which of the qualities below describe this character.

Bullying Leader:

_____ bossy

_____ aggressive

_____ has a short temper

_____ refuses to follow rules

_____ is more attractive than those (s)he is mean to

_____ is physically stronger than those (s)he is mean to

_____ is more popular and confident than those (s)he bullies

Bullying Follower:

_____ thinks bullying is fun

_____ admires leaders of bullying

_____ lacks confidence and assertiveness skills

_____ does not feel responsible for their own behavior

_____ thinks they won't get in trouble for being disrespectful

_____ thinks that bullying leaders become popular by acting mean

_____ thinks that joining in on bullying will make him or herself more popular

_____ believes that those who are bullied deserve to be treated with disrespect

3. Is the character a bullying leader or follower? _____

Discussion: Who Bullies?

Ask children the following questions. Instruct them to not use children's real names during this conversation. Advise them to communicate privately later if they need to.

1. Describe characters you have read about in books who bullied others.
   a. How did they act?
   b. Were they leaders or followers?

2. Describe people you have seen in TV shows, movies or video games that had bullying behavior.
   a. How did they act?
   b. Were they leaders or followers?

3. Are friends sometimes mean?
   a. In what ways?

4. How does gossip hurt people?

5. Have you ever heard of one child trying to take another child's friends away?
   a. If yes, can you describe the situation without using real names?

6. *Girls who bully are more indirect than boys who bully are.*
   a. Raise your hand if you
      • think this is true
      • think this is not true
      • don't know
   b. Why did you answer true or not true?
   c. After hearing what your fellow students think, has anyone who said they didn't know, changed your mind?

7. *Laughing at someone who doesn't want to be laughed at is an example of disrespect.*
   a. Raise your hand if you
      • agree with this statement
      • disagree
   b. Why did you agree or disagree?

8. *It is fun to treat another student with disrespect.*
   a. Raise your hand if you
      • agree with this statement
      • disagree
   b. Why did you agree or disagree?

9. *Sometimes a student deserves to be treated with disrespect.* How many agree with this statement? How many disagree? Why do you agree or disagree?

10. *Sometimes a student deserves to be bullied.* How many agree with this statement? How many disagree? Why do you agree or disagree?

LEADERS OF BULLYING

Julia is an example of a leader of bullying. In fifth grade she started a group at her school called the "Jewels" and invited five girls to become members. Julia acted like there was something wrong with any girl who wasn't one of the "Jewels. The members of her group did the same thing. Secretly Julia thought the girls in her group were dumb because they did whatever she told them to do. She knew that the "Jewels" put other girls down so that they themselves could look perfect. Julia loved it that unpopular girls feared her and her group and wished they too could be members of the "Jewels".

1. Complete assignment a or b.

    a. Write a story about Julia. Describe what happened to her when she was younger that might have caused her to become a leader of bullying.

    b. Write a story about Ryon (or Carlos). Describe what happened to him when he was younger that might have caused him to become a leader of bullying.

RESPECT AGREEMENT

1. This activity requires at least two people, a group or a classroom.

2. Each person in the pair, group, or class talks about how they want to be treated by others at school. Use the *Respect & Disrespect* handout for ideas.

3. Choose three ways that you and your partner, group, or class agree to try to treat each other with respect. List them below.

We agree to try to treat each other with respect by:

a. _____

_____

_____

b. _____

_____

_____

c. _____

_____

_____

4. Each person who helped create the agreement signs it.

Signatures

_____

_____

_____

FUR

Who Is Bullied?

Objectives

- To provide students with a wide variety of illustrations of how they can assertively stick up for themselves when treated with disrespect.

- To explore the concept of bullying.

- To identify characteristics of those who are bullied.

- To help students develop assertive communication skills.

Chapter Summary, *Avery Quinn: Erupting*

Mr. Sergio teaches Avery how to ask questions beginning with "W" as another way to respond to bullying. Avery still has not informed his father. Mr. Sergio still has not taken actions to intervene on Avery's behalf. (The story is set up this way so that your students can learn, discuss and practice different assertiveness strategies as ways to respond to disrespect.)

Avery bumbles along, trying to act more assertive. Then three things happen. The bullying becomes worse, the bus driver intervenes, and for the first time a student on the bus gives Avery some support.

Suggestion for Success

Trying to get the leaders of bullying and those they bully to change is a less effective approach than helping the majority of students in between to change what they do. This curriculum helps motivate students who are not bullied to stop supporting the children who bully and support those who are bullied instead.

Activities

Avery Quinn: Erupting
- a. Read *Avery Quinn: Erupting* aloud to the class.
- b. Use the Chapter Discussion questions to stimulate a class conversation about the chapter.
1. "W" Questions
   - a. Distribute the Handout: *Using "W" Questions: Twana & Malcolm* for each student to complete.
   - b. Go through each question so children can share their answers. Then they turn in their completed work.
   - c. Ask children to raise their hands if they would feel
     - comfortable using a "W" question if someone treated them with disrespect? (Record the number.)
     - uncomfortable using a "W" question. (Record the number.)

2. Role-play: "W" Questions #1

Involve small groups or the whole class in role-plays. Use approach a or b.

   a. Divide students into pairs. Distribute the Handout: *"W" Questions #1*.

   • Explain that one student will read the disrespectful statements and the other will pretend to be Avery speaking up for himself. Everyone speaking as Avery should stand tall, pull their shoulders back, hold their head high, and talk calmly without yelling.

   • After students have done the role-play once, they switch places. The one who played Avery first now reads the disrespectful statement and vice versa.

   • De-brief. Children call each other by their real names and ask each other how it felt to read the disrespectful and assertive statements.

   b. A simpler approach, and if the group needs more structure, is for the teacher to read the disrespectful statements and one at a time, or the whole group together, give the assertive response.

   • De-brief. Call students by their real names and ask them how it felt to say the assertive responses.

3. Homework: "W" questions

   a. Students repeat the *"W" Questions #1* activity with a family member, friend, neighbor, or teacher and complete the *"W" Questions #2* handout.

   b. Ask students to raise their hands if they would feel

   • comfortable using a "W" question if someone treated them with disrespect? (Record the number.)

   • uncomfortable using a "W" question. (Record the number.)

   c. Compare these numbers to the last time you asked this question, to see if, after having practiced, students feel more or less comfortable using "W" questions.

4. Homework: Erupting & Cool

   a. Distribute the Handout: *Erupting & Cool* for students to complete.

   b. Ask for volunteers to share their responses the the Handout: *Erupting & Cool*. Afterwards children turn in their completed handouts.

5. Richard—a real-life example of a child having *Erupting* behaviors and working hard to transform them into *Cool* behaviors.

   a. Use the Handout: *Richard* as a supplement to any of the activities in this section.

6. Homework: Who Is Bullied?

   a. Distribute the Handout: *Who Is Bullied?* for students to read and complete.

   b. Ask each student to report to the class their answers to the questions on the Handout: *Who Is Bullied?*. Afterwards children turn in their completed work.

7. Journal

   Students respond to the following questions in their journals.

   a. Without using any real names, describe the behavior of someone you have seen in our school who is treated with disrespect or bullied. Was their behavior erupting or cool?

   b. How do you think Avery will act in the future?

Avery Quinn: *Erupting*

When I got to the gym Mr. Sergio was jumping rope really fast. He called to me across the gym, "Today is my volcano lesson."

"Know how volcanoes got their name?" I asked as I walked toward him.

"No," he said.

"After Vulcan."

Mr. Sergio stopped jumping rope. "Who is Vulcan?"

"The Roman's God of Fire," I said.

"Cool," said Mr.Sergio.

"Ever hear of Vesuvius?" I asked.

"The mountain in Pompeii that blew up?"

"Yep. The people who couldn't escape, and the buildings, got covered by hot rocks that were inside the mountain."

Mr. Sergio reached into his pocket and pulled out a small ball of yarn. "I learned about Pompeii when I was your age," he said, tossing me the yarn ball. "We know a lot about what happened the day Vesuvius erupted, because a boy who lived across the bay from Pompeii, wrote down everything he saw."

"That was Pliny the Younger," I said, easily catching the ball and throwing it back.

"Pliny," Mr. Sergio repeated, "how'd you like a name like that?"

"I'd change it," I said.

"To what, Pli?"

"Maybe Ny."

"That works," said Mr. Sergio. "Have you ever thought of changing your name?"

"What do you mean?" I asked.

"To one that kids wouldn't pick on," answered Mr. Sergio.

"I'm named after my mother's father," I said.

There was a pause. Mr. Sergio must have sensed the importance of what I had said. He nodded.

"There are more volcanoes under water than on land," I said.

"Really?"

"Volcanoes under water are called *hot spots,*" I told him.

"Weren't the Hawaiian Islands formed from volcanoes that erupted in the Pacific Ocean?"

"Yeah."

"Getting bullied is like being in a *hot spot,*" said Mr. Sergio. "Emotions can heat up and explode. But bully blocking is about keeping your cool."

Keeping my cool, I thought, *I could do that at the river, but not at school.*

"Another way to assert yourself is to ask "W" questions—*what, why, and who.*" He hopped from one foot to the other. "What are you doing? Why are you doing that? Who told you that? What makes you think I'm that way? Why would you say that? Who are you? What's up? Why are you picking on me? What is your name? Why are you acting that way? Who are you? What time is it? Why should I? Who told you that? What are you talking about? Why do you think that's true? Who cares?

I must have looked puzzled.

"Let's give it a try," said Mr. Sergio. "Talk like the kids who bully you and I'll show you how."

"Hey, knock knees," I said grinning like Carlos.

"What makes you think that's my name?" asked Mr. Sergio.

I thought, *that sounded pretty good.*

Making my face look as angry as I could, I asked, "Hiding in the nurse's office?"

"Why should I?" asked Mr. Sergio.

I tried another one. "Are you giving me the evil eye?"

"Who does that?"

Asking questions seemed difficult. Mr. Sergio did it easily, but not me.

Thursday morning Ryon sat across the aisle from me in the second row. I glanced at his light blue soccer shirt and told myself, *I'm going to be courageous.*

"What's in your pocket, rocket?" Ryon asked.

"None of your business," I said. I couldn't believe it was me talking.

"Oh yeah?"

My throat was dry. I could hardly speak. "Yeah."

"Want to fight?"

My courage was fading fast. "I don't."

"You wish you could."

That was the most I had spoken up for myself to him.

"I'll show you how," he said.

I turned away.

"Too afraid. You know you couldn't win. Don't have any muscles. Your legs would give out. What can you do anyway with only one arm?" He went on and on, egging me to respond.

I'm not letting him win. I'm not letting him. I'm not, I told myself over and over again until finally the bus pulled into the school parking lot. Ryon couldn't wait for me to get off the bus. He flew down the steps and onto the field in front of the school.

Just as I joined the line of students waiting to go inside, Carlos stepped behind me.

"You're too slow," he complained.

Go away, I wanted to say, but he was so much bigger than I was.

"Let me help you," said Carlos, poking a finger in my back.

He kept poking me until we reached the stairs. I headed toward the fourth grade classrooms. Enzo was at the end of the hall doing some kind of crazy tap dance. A group of kids stood around him. I wanted to join them and laugh at Enzo like everybody else. But no.

"Dance with me Quinny," he said when he saw me.

Once more he ruined my chances of fitting in.

"Stop annoying me," I said in an angry voice.

"No sense of humor," teased Enzo.

Marcella piped in. "Queeny. Quinny," she sang.

"Cut it out," I snapped.

At recess Mr. Sergio and I played volleyball with balloons and a low net, and made up more *what, who, why* skits.

I pretended to be Carlos. "Let me help you," I said, poking Mr. Sergio in the back.

"Why are you touching me?" he asked.

I kept poking him.

"What's wrong with your finger?" he calmly asked.

I pretended to be Enzo dancing around. "Dance with me queeny."

"Who would think I'd want to do that?" asked Mr. Sergio.

"But," I protested, " Enzo would say something like, because you're a queer, oh, I meant queen, oh sorry, I meant Quinn."

"Sometimes yes, but other times it just might slow him down," said Mr. Sergio. "Doesn't slowing down come before stopping?"

"I guess," I said, not sure if I really agreed.

That afternoon, Ryon was not on the bus. He wasn't there the next day either. I thought, *maybe he was bitten by a dear tick on the soccer field and has Lyme disease. Then he'd be too weak to bother me. He'd have to stay out of school for a long time. I imagined problems the rest of them could have. Bird flu virus. West Nile virus. Eastern Equine Encephalitis. Tarantula, rattlesnake, and Black Widow Spider bites. Rabies.*

When I got off the bus Carlos greeted me with an extra wide grin.

"Happy to see me?" he asked, glancing at his audience of fifth grade girls.

"No," I said.

"Look who has a voice," he exclaimed to the girls.

Why do they have such a crush on him? I wondered.

"Whoa. Whoa," said Enzo and Marcella.

Carlos got so close to me that I thought his eyelashes were going to brush my face. "Say more," he said.

But I didn't.

As I limped down the hall, Enzo and Marcella stuck close to me, making noises that sounded like farts.

"Why are you doing that?" I asked.

"To be or not to be, that is the question," Enzo replied. "Ours is not to wonder why."

I felt stupid. If only I could joke back. "Buzz off," I said to Marcella before she had a chance to speak. I felt better about that.

"I asked Enzo a *why* question," I told Mr. Sergio while we were warming up.

"How did it go?"

"Not so good."

"It was your first time," he said.

We practiced using "W" questions some more, but I wasn't sure it would do me any good.

On the bus ride home I imagined Ryon lying on the ground covered with mosquitoes, spiders and snakes and pecked at by turkey vultures. A gorilla squeezed Marcella to death. Elephants stampeded Enzo. A Tyrannosaurus Rex chewed Carlos to pieces. I held my hand over my mouth to hide my smile.

The next morning Ryon wasn't on the bus. I looked out the window and daydreamed. It was as if I wasn't even there. I was still in sort of a daze when I ran into Carlos.

"Watch your step, Captain Hook," he said, pretending to slash me with an invisible sword.

I was halfway surprised to see him alive.

"Go away," I said. *Yikes!* I thought. *Did I really say that?* I wished I could take it back.

"So you're a tough guy?" exclaimed Carlos, acting like he was a boxer getting ready to throw a punch.

"So tough," echoed Enzo.

"Tough," said Marcella.

I held my breath.

Carlos turned to his girl friends and said, "I'll teach him not to talk to me like that," then facing me, "Don't you know who you are?"

I thought to myself, *no, who am I?* "What do you mean?" I asked.

"Ha," laughed Carlos.

"Ha. Ha. Ha. Ha," laughed Enzo and Marcella as they followed me down the hall laughing and waving their hands in front of my face.

"Don't you have something better to do?" I said, pushing their hands away.

"Nope," said Enzo.

"Nope," agreed Marcella.

"I asked Carlos a *what* question, but he just laughed," I told Mr. Sergio later at recess.

"Good for you."

"I told him to go away."

"I bet you surprised him."

"Yeah, me too."

That afternoon, during *Drop Everything and Read* time, I went to the boys' bathroom. Carlos was washing his hands at a sink. He wasn't supposed to be there. Fifth graders had their own bathroom upstairs. No one else was around. I imagined a flood coming out of the faucet and drowning him.

"Get out of here," yelled Carlos. He wasn't smiling.

"Why are you mean to me?" I asked. It felt strong to speak to him like that.

He just stood there looking at me, then said, "Because," and left.

I smiled the whole time on the bus ride home that afternoon. I felt proud of myself for speaking up to Carlos.

The next morning in the sky outside our cabin, were hundreds of tree swallows. *Flying away,* I thought. Standing at the bus stop I crossed two fingers on my right hand and made a wish that Ryon had flown away too. But no. There he was in his yellow and red soccer uniform sitting right behind my usual seat. *Gee,* I thought, *he doesn't even look sick.*

Ryon rubbed his hands together, and said, in an evil sounding voice, "If it isn't my little pawn."

I faced him, "Why are you picking on me?"

"It's fun. You're such a wimp."

I looked away.

"Your father is too."

There was a terrible taste in my mouth. I felt like throwing up. I couldn't stand it when Ryon said something about my parents. I sat down. He blew on the back of my neck. I didn't move. He pushed me forward with his hand. I pulled away.

"What are you doing?" I hissed.

Ryon grabbed my jacket.

"Let go," I cried, slapping his hand away.

He spit on me. I felt like Vesuvius, ready to explode.

"Quit it," I yelled.

He took hold of my shoulders and shook me.

"Stop," I heard somebody on the bus shout.

"Get your hands off me," I screamed.

"No way," Ryon screamed back.

"Stop, Ryon. Stop," somebody yelled again.

"What's going on?" grumbled the bus driver.

No one answered. Ryon let go. I wiped his spit off my jacket. The rest of the ride was quiet, except for my thundering heart. I kept hearing the words, "Stop Ryon, Stop. Stop Ryon, Stop." I couldn't believe it. *Was someone trying to help?*

Chapter Discussion

Discuss *Avery Quinn: Erupting.* Ask students not to use children's real names during this conversation. Advise them to communicate privately later if they need to.

1. How is Avery feeling now?

2. How is he changing?

3. Will Avery's sticking up for himself cause the bullying to stop? Why or why not?

4. What do *erupting* behaviors look like? Sound like?

5. What do *cool* behaviors look like? Sound like?

6. When you want to keep your cool what do you do?

7. What does it feel like to be the last person picked for a game or group activity?

Create a chart for the class to see, with the letters a–h in a vertical line corresponding with two columns, one titled *yes* and the other *no*. After asking each question below, record on the chart the number of hands raised. When you complete letter h, encourage students to come up with their own questions to ask the group.

8. Raise your hand if you have seen someone teased because
   a. of their name?
   b. of how they looked?
   c. of how much they weighed?
   d. they wore glasses?
   e. they ate food that was different?
   f. they were short?
   g. they were tall?
   h. they couldn't read aloud very well?

9. What do you think students get teased about the most at our school?

USING "W" QUESTIONS: TWANA & MALCOLM

Twana—Courage in My Life

I remember when I was in K1 some kids in the 5th grade used to bother me on the afternoon bus and at school whenever they saw me. They called me some mean and nasty names, I'd rather not say. Sometimes they even used hand gestures toward me.

This went on for most of the year. I did not tell my mother because they said if I did they would beat me up. The only one I told was my best friend, Trina. I made her pinky promise that she would not tell anyone.

One day I decided to tell them to leave me alone. As I walked toward them, my hands got sweaty, my throat got dry, and my legs felt like they were going to shake themselves off. I was determined to stand up for myself. I asked them why they picked on me. Why did they not pick on someone their own size? I told them how much they hurt my feelings. They said sorry to me. I guess they did not realize how bad they had hurt my feelings. They never bothered me again. I finally told my mother and she was very proud of me.

I am glad that I stood up for myself and had courage. Now any time I see them I remember that time I was courageous.

The Courage of Boston's Children, Volume XII, The Max Warburg Courage Curriculum and the Boston Public Schools, Houghton Mifflin Company, 2003.

Malcolm—Courage in My Life

I have had a lot of courageous times in my life, but there's one moment that I will never forget.

The first day of school in second grade things were going fine. Then the teacher started taking attendance and calling out people's names.

"Durell," she called out.

"Here."

"Ruben."

"Here."

"Malcolm. Malcolm?"

I guess I did not hear my name being called.

"CAMPBELL! MALCOLM CAMPBELL?" she yelled out.

HAAAAAAAAAAAA! The whole class laughed as I raised my hand and told the teacher I was present. I felt like blowing up! I was so angry. Even my friends were laughing. They started calling me "Campbell Soup."

Two months passed and almost everybody stopped calling me Campbell Soup. But one boy, Keith, did not stop. He kept calling me names and pushing me.

One day he punched me. I felt terrible because he was picking on me. He took it too far. I knew that it would only get worse. All night I was thinking that I should tell a teacher. I had a big decision to make.

When I got to school that morning, I went up to Keith. I was scared that he might hit me. I knew that I had to tell him how I felt. I asked him why he kept picking on me. He told me that he was just having fun and that he didn't know that it was hurting my feelings. He told me he was sorry. We became friends. I was courageous because I faced the class bully. Even though I was scared I faced my fear. Sometimes you need to stand up for what is right, even though you are scared.

The Courage of Boston's Children, Volume XII, The Max Warburg Courage Curriculum and the Boston Public Schools, Houghton Mifflin Company, 2003.

1. What questions beginning with the letter "W" did Twana and Malcolm use to speak up for themselves?

_____

_____

_____

_____

2. When is it a good idea to tell someone how you feel, if that person is treating you with disrespect? When is it not a good idea?

_____

_____

_____

_____

3. Is it possible for a person who bullies to become good friends with someone he or she bullied? Explain your answer.

_____

_____

_____

_____

"W" QUESTIONS #1

This activity requires at least two people: one to read the disrespectful statements and the other to pretend to be Avery speaking up for himself.

When you pretend to be Avery stand tall, pull your shoulders back, hold your head high, and speak in a calm voice without yelling.

Disrespectful Statements	**Assertive Responses**
Hey, knock-knees.	What makes you think that's my name?
Hiding in the nurse's office?	Why should I?
Are you giving me the evil eye?	Who does that?
Let me help you. (ha, ha)	What are you doing?
Get out of here.	Why are you mean to me?
Dance with me queeny.	What makes you think I'd want to do that?
If it isn't my little pawn.	Who are you to pick on me?

After completing this assignment, de-brief by calling each other by your real names and asking your partner...

• What did it feel like to read the disrespectful statements?
• What did it feel like to read the assertive statements?

"W" QUESTIONS #2

Repeat the *"W" Questions #1* activity with a family member, friend, neighbor, or teacher. When you are done, de-brief. Ask your partner how it felt for him or her to read the disrespectful and assertive statements. Record their answers.

1. How did it feel to read the disrespectful statements?

_____

_____

_____

_____

2. How did it feel to read the assertive statements?

_____

_____

_____

_____

3. Circle the correct description of your partner.

Family member: mother   father   sister   brother   grandparent   aunt   uncle   other

friend   neighbor   teacher

ERUPTING & COOL

1. Write about a time when you were in a conflict with someone and your behavior was *erupting*.

_____

_____

_____

_____

_____

_____

_____

_____

2. Write about a time when you were in a conflict with someone and your behavior was *cool*.

_____

_____

_____

_____

_____

_____

_____

_____

_____

RICHARD

Courage in My Life

...In this essay, I want to write about one of the definitions of what courage means to me. To me, courage means to have the guts to change. I have a bad habit of my own. During previous school years, I seemed to lash out at anybody who wanted to make a joke about me. I knew I had a problem with my temper and was easily provoked. As a result, I got easily angry and into an edgy mood. I would start getting frustrated and would hurt other people's feelings. This leads to hurting some of my classmates' feelings and makes me perceived to be an unfriendly person.

One of the times I lashed out at a person was in October 2006. I was feeling pretty good. We had a good class and were relaxing around the cafeteria. I was chatting with my friends, until a young boy interrupted our conversation. Coming right up to my face, he yelled, "I bet you don't have enough money to buy your lunch! Your family is poorer than the poorest beggar in the world. You'll be stuck in poverty forever and ever and ever!"

Looking back, I knew what I did was wrong, but I was blind to all faults and reasons. I jumped right out of my seat, anger blazing in my eyes and, ignoring everyone yelling for me to stop, I leapt right on him, slamming his body onto the floor. He started to say, "No more," and suddenly, I stopped. I realized that if either of us got hurt, we would get in trouble together and my parents would have to come to school to pick me up. I told my mom what happened and that incident turned into a long lecture from my mother about me and my temper.

During these past Christmas holidays, I decided to change. At that time, I was thinking about changing my notorious, despicable temper into a friendly non-bubbling temper, because I was destroying my friends and family with it. Now, I am beginning to work on it like it was a homework assignment. Since then, I've had many improvements. I know there will be lots of room for improvement in the future. But despite all obstacles, I have complete faith in myself to improve my temper.

The Courage of Boston's Children, Volumn XVII, The Max Warburg Courage Curriculum, Inc. and the Boston Public Schools, Northeastern University, 2008.

1. List behaviors mentioned in Richard's essay that were...

Physically Disrespectful

_____

_____

_____

Non-verbally Disrespectful

_____

_____

_____

Verbally Disrespectful

_____

_____

_____

Assertive

_____

_____

_____

2. Put an E next to the actions listed above that were *erupting*.

3. List any *cool* behaviors that were described in Richard's essay.

_____   _____

_____   _____

_____   _____

WHO IS BULLIED?

Many children who are bullied at school have something in common with Avery. They:
- lack confidence,
- have few or no friends,
- don't like to be aggressive or mean, and
- have shy, quiet, and nervous personalities.

Their behavior is passive.

If they are boys, they may be physically weaker and less coordinated than others their age.

If they are girls, they may be less attractive than others their age.

Students who bully think the children they pick on are not "good enough" or don't "fit in." They might make fun of them because they are over-weight, overly skinny, tall, short, dress in a non-trendy way, or not speak English well. However there are children who look, dress, act and speak "differently", but do *not* get bullied. These children tend to have confidence, act assertively, and be supported by other students and adults. They may also have relaxed and easy-going personalities.

Shirley Temple Wong is a child who is bullied. She is the main character in the fictional book, *In the Year of the Boar and Jackie Robinson*. Shirley moves to the United States from China when she is nine years old. She does not understand the customs of modern American culture or much English. She has a shy, quiet and nervous personality, is not confident, and has no friends. It is not her nature to be aggressive or mean.

Classmates laugh at Shirley. They whisper when she passes, call her "teacher's dog," and won't let her play baseball with them. Shirley feels bad about herself, thinks she is a failure, and doesn't know how to stick up for herself or ask for help.

Some children who are bullied at school are like Avery and Shirley in that they:
- lack confidence,
- have few or no friends, and
- have nervous personalities.

If they are boys, they may be physically weaker and less coordinated than others their age.

If they are girls, they may be less attractive than others their age.

However they may also:
- act younger than their age,
- do things that irritate people,
- have difficulty paying attention, and
- have behavior that is aggressive, hyperactive, and clumsy.

An example of a child who acts like this is Zinkoff, the main character in the book *Loser* by Jerry Spinelli. He is physically weaker and less coordinated than boys his age are. He is hyperactive and clumsy. Children and teachers find him irritating. Zinkoff talks too loud, gets too excited, laughs too much, and frequently trips and falls on his face. No one wants to be his friend. Children who bully, laugh at and make fun of Zinkoff. They call him *loser*. Zinkoff however, does not act aggressively or bully anyone smaller than himself.

Choose a character in a book, or someone who you saw in a TV show, movie, or video game, that was bullied.

1. Name of the character. _____

2. Title of the book, TV show, movie or video game. _____

3. Check the qualities below that describe this character.

_____ lacks confidence

_____ has passive behavior

_____ has few or no friends

_____ is hyperactive and clumsy

_____ has difficulty paying attention

_____ does things that irritate people

_____ is less attractive than other girls

_____ acts younger than kids the same age

_____ doesn't like to be mean or aggressive

_____ bullies children weaker than themselves

_____ has a shy, quiet, and nervous personality

_____ acts aggressively when treated with disrespect

_____ is physically weaker and less coordinated than other boys

FIVE

Who Silently Watches Bullying?

Objectives

- To explore the concept of bullying.

- To provide students with a wide variety of illustrations of how they can respectfully stick up for themselves when treated with disrespect.

- To identify the characteristics of those who silently watch bullying at school and the role they play in encouraging bullies.

- To explore ways to successfully keep *Respect Agreements*.

- To help students develop assertive communication skills.

- To explore ways students can help stop bullying at school.

Chapter Summaries, *Avery Quinn: Mudslide* and *Avery Quinn: Stone Wall*

A conflict arises between Mr. Sergio and Avery, which they resolve. Mr. Sergio teaches Avery a bully blocking technique called *Stonewalling*. When the bullying escalates again, Avery handles the situation well and receives additional peer support.

Suggestion for Success

Note that the topic *Who Silently Watches Bullying?* is introduced at the same time a peer helper appears in the story of *Avery Quinn*. Since the core objective of this curriculum is to encourage the silent majority to become more of a helping majority, this focused topic is very important to include.

Activities

Avery Quinn: Mudslide and *Stone Wall*

a. Read the two chapters *Avery Quinn: Mudslide* and *Stone Wall* aloud to the class.

b. Use the Chapter Discussion questions to stimulate conversation about the chapters.

Select from the recommended activities below, especially those in bold.

1. Role-plays: Stone Wall #1

Use approach a or b.

a. Divide students into pairs.

- Distribute the Handout: *Stone Wall #1*.

- Explain that one student will read the disrespectful statements and the other will pretend to be Avery speaking up for himself. Everyone who speaks as Avery should stand tall, pull their shoulders back, hold their head high, take a breath, and speak calmly without yelling.

- After students have done the role-play once, they switch places. The one who played Avery first now reads the disrespectful statement and vice versa.
- De-brief. Students call each other by their real names and ask each other how it felt to read the disrespectful and assertive statements.

b. A simpler and quicker approach, and if the group needs more structure, is for the teacher to read the disrespectful statements and one at a time, or the whole group together, give the assertive responses. Then de-brief. Call children by their real names. Ask them how it felt to say the assertive responses.

2. Homework: Stone Wall #2

a. Students repeat the *Stone Wall #1* activity with a family member, friend, neighbor, or teacher and complete the *Stone Wall #2* handout.

3. Who Silently Watches Bullying?

a. Distribute the Handout: *Who Silently Watches Bullying?* for students to read and complete.

b. Read aloud the questions from the handout. Ask students to share their responses. Afterwards children turn in their completed work.

4. Respect Agreement Meeting

Conduct *Respect Agreement Meetings* weekly throughout the school year to discuss how to successfully keep *Respect Agreements*.

a. Reunite the pairs or small groups who created *Respect Agreements* together, or do this activity with the whole class. You will need copies of the *Respect Agreements* that were previously created in section Three.

b. Each pair/group/class discusses and completes the *Respect Agreement Meeting* handout.

c. If you haven't already, create a classroom *Respect Agreement* (see Activities, section Three).

5. Journal

Students respond to the following questions in their journals.

a. Why do you think students silently watch Avery being bullied and do nothing to help him?

b. What might happen if the children at Parker Elementary School stopped being silent and assertively stood up for Avery instead?

Avery Quinn: *Mudslide*

I was glad to see Mr. Sergio at recess. He was balancing a beach ball on the top of his head.

"Ryon spit on me."

"Then what happened?"

"We were screaming. The bus driver told us to stop."

"And?"

"Ryon left me alone."

"Thanks to the bus driver," said Mr. Sergio.

"Somebody else too."

"Who?"

"I don't know."

"A potential friend?"

I shrugged my shoulders.

"Stay there," instructed Mr. Sergio. He walked a distance away from me and kicked the beach ball into the air. I captured it and kicked it back.

"What if Ryon does that again?"

"We could tell Mrs. Shane," said Mr. Sergio.

"What could she do?"

"She's in charge of who rides the bus."

"If Ryon got kicked off the bus, he'd get back at me worse."

"Maybe yes, maybe no."

"Cuz I'm speaking up, he's hurting me more."

"Things can get worse before they get better." The beach ball rolled past me.

"You didn't tell me that."

"Sorry," he said.

There was a long silence. Mr. Sergio walked behind me, picked up the beach ball and tossed it my way. I caught it but didn't pass it back. He touched his toes. Shook out his hands. I glared at the door. He motioned for me to pass the ball.

Why do I trust you? I thought.

I hurried out of the gym. He didn't try to stop me. I moved as fast as I could past the locker room next to the gym. The next closest boys' bathroom was next to my classroom at the other end of the hall. I thought, *what if someone sees me and asks what I'm doing?* My heart raced. *Will Mr. Sergio report me to my teacher?* I heard voices. My hands were hot and sweaty. As I inched forward I thought, *if only I could run.*

The voices grew louder just as I reached the bathroom. I dove inside planning to hide in a stall until my class returned. I saw in the mirror that my cheeks were flushed, just like Ryon's. *Now what?* I asked the face.

Avery Quinn: *Stone Wall*

I did not want to go to recess the next day and I didn't have any other option, so I went to the gym. "Did you report me to my teacher?" I asked.

"No," answered Mr. Sergio.

"To the Principal?"

"No," he said.

"My father?"

"No, no one," he said.

"I don't think those "W" questions do any good," I blurted out.

"I didn't either when I first started speaking up."

There was a long silence. The beach ball was against the wall. I got it and kicked it to Mr. Sergio. He rolled it toward me and then, with his feet, tried to steal it back.

"How much longer is this going to take?" I asked, trying to not let him get possession of the ball.

"What?"

"Before they stop being mean?"

"I don't know," he said, stealing the ball from me.

"What if I just gave up?"

"And then?"

"Give them detention or something," I said.

"If you want I will, but with your physical challenges, Avery, I think you will still need to know how to stick up for yourself. What if you hung in there a bit longer? I think you're near a *tipping point*."

"What's that?"

He spread his arms wide in the air. "A time of dramatic change."

"For better or worse?" I asked.

"For the better," he said.

Somehow his saying that made me feel hopeful. I stole the beach ball back.

"If Ryon touches me again, maybe we can tell the principal," I said.

Mr. Sergio nodded.

"I was going to talk about tornadoes today," I said.

"Want to say more about what happened the other day on the bus?"

I shook my head. I was thinking about the fact that I hadn't told my father yet about being bullied. *He has so much on his mind,* I thought. *I don't want him worrying about this too.*

"Tornadoes are the most powerful storms on earth," I said. "They are about a mile wide at the top, but there was one once that was three hundred miles wide. Tornadoes can be as tall as eight hundred feet and travel as fast as three hundred miles per hour. In China once, thirteen kids got picked up by a tornado and were carried for twelve miles. None of them were hurt."

"Really?" asked Mr. Sergio.

"I wish Ryon, Carlos, Enzo, and Marcella would get carried off by a tornado."

"Until that happens, want to learn another skill?"

"I guess."

"Stonewalling," began Mr. Sergio. "Act like a stone wall. Hold your position. Don't budge an inch. Repeat the same words again and again. Wear your opponent down." He threw the beach ball into a corner of his office and grabbed a soft green-striped Frisbee off of a shelf. He spun the Frisbee on the tip of the index finger of his right hand.

"Use *stonewalling* or act like a *broken record*," he said. "Before there were tapes, CDs, DVDs, computers and iPods, people listened to records."

He spun the Frisbee faster and faster.

"If the surface of a record got scratched, the needle on the record player stayed in one place and played the same word over and over and over."

He spun the Frisbee slowly.

"When a student talks to you in a hurtful way, be like a *broken record*. Give the exact same response like So. So. So. So. So or Nope. Nope. Nope. Nope. Nope."

For several days Ryon acted like I wasn't riding the bus. I imagined that he was a lion, crouched low, ready to pounce. I didn't see Carlos with his group of girls, Enzo, or Marcella either. *A pride of lions, going for the kill*, I thought, *and I, a lone animal, not part of a herd. Easy prey!*

I got lazy about doing physical exercises with Mr. Sergio and just wanted to practice defending myself by being a *broken record* or stone wall.

One afternoon on my way to the bus Ryon, Carlos, Enzo and Marcella cornered me. I felt like a fish in a bowl surrounded by four hungry, sharp-clawed cats. I hunched my shoulders and studied the ground.

"We don't like you," said Carlos.

"So," I meekly replied.

Ryon spoke in a very loud voice, "Girly boy."

"So," I said almost choking.

My head was spinning as if I was swimming around and around inside a bowl. I thought, *if I were a shark I'd devour all four of them in one gulp.*

"Cripple," taunted Carlos.

"So," I hissed.

Enzo pointed at my left leg.

"You walk funny," he dramatically sang.

I gave him a stony look and said, "So."

"Can't you say anything but so?" complained Marcella.

"Ny," I said as I squeezed past her and Carlos's girl friends, and climbed up the bus steps.

When Ryon passed me on his way to the back of the bus he said, "I'm getting as far away as I can from this So and So."

I watched him hurry away. I was cool and still like a stone wall. A boy with a yellow baseball cap, with the letters WWF on it, gave me a *thumbs-up* sign.

Chapter Discussion

Discuss *Avery Quinn: Mud Slide* and *Avery Quinn: Stone Wall*. Ask students to refrain from using children's real names when discussing bullying. Advise them to communicate privately later if they need to.

1. Why hasn't Avery told his father about being bullied?

2. Do you think you could use *stonewalling* if someone in your school repeatedly treated you with disrespect?

3. How is Avery feeling now?

4. How is he changing?

5. Raise your hand if you think that the boy wearing the yellow baseball cap is trying to help Avery? Explain your answer.

STONE WALL #1

This activity requires at least two people: one person reads the disrespectful statements and the other pretends to be Avery speaking up for himself.

When you pretend to be Avery stand tall, pull your shoulders back, hold your head high, take a deep breath, and speak in a calm voice without yelling.

Disrespectful Statements	Assertive Responses
We don't like you.	So.
Girly boy.	So.
Cripple.	So.
You walk funny.	So.
Cry baby.	So.
Knock knees.	So.
Slow poke.	So.
If it isn't the sportsman Avery Quinn.	So.
Avery is a girl.	So.
Pirate, where's your hook?	So.
What's wrong with you?	So.
Too chicken?	So.

After completing this assignment, de-brief by calling each other by your real names and ask your partner...

• What did it feel like to read the disrespectful statements?
• What did it feel like to read the assertive statements?

STONE WALL #2

Repeat the *Stone Wall #1* activity with a family member, friend, neighbor, or teacher. When you are done, de-brief. Ask your partner how it felt to read the disrespectful and assertive statements. Record their answers.

1. How did it feel to read the disrespectful statements?

_____

_____

_____

_____

_____

2. How did it feel to read the assertive statements?

_____

_____

_____

_____

_____

3. Circle the correct description of your partner.

Family member: mother   father   sister   brother   grandparent   aunt   uncle   other

friend   neighbor   teacher

WHO SILENTLY WATCHES BULLYING?

Most of the time when bullying happens at school other children silently watch. These students don't join in with the bullying like followers do, but they don't help those who are bullied either.

Sometimes those who silently watch are too scared to stick up for others. They don't want to get bullied themselves, or called a *tattletale, snitch, fink, squealer,* or *rat.* Sometimes they don't understand how hurtful the bullying is, or think someone else will take responsibility to help. Other times they don't want to get involved, think those who are bullied deserve it, or, if the person is not a friend of theirs, don't care. There are also children who want to help those who are bullied but have no idea what to do.

When students silently watch bullying and don't try to help, the children who bully get so much support that it is hard for them to change.

Maddie, the main character in the book *The Hundred Dresses* by Eleanor Estes, silently watches her best friend Peggy tease Wanda, a classmate with no friends. Other girls join in. They mock and laugh at Wanda and say mean things about her behind her back. Maddie is part of the group but doesn't join in on the teasing. She feels uncomfortable and imagines how Wanda must feel. She wants to say, "Stop it. This girl is just a girl like you are," but is afraid her friends will turn on her. Maddie doesn't even have the courage to ask her best friend Peggy in private to stop being so cruel. She convinces herself that Peggy isn't really unkind and that Wanda deserves to be treated with disrespect.

Wilnord, a sixth grader in the Boston Public Schools, Boston, MA wrote this *Courage in My Life* essay about how in fifth grade he watched his friends bully a new student at school and decided he had to do something to help.

You could use the word courage in many different ways, but my definition of courage is to stand up and take steps one by one until you reach your goal. One time in elementary school I tried to stand up for something that was right, which made me lose my friends. I didn't know it was going to be so hard.

In the fifth grade I hung out with a group of boys. We did a lot of things together. At recess we played football together. On the weekends we called each other and made plans to get together. I considered them my good friends, letting them borrow my things and telling them secrets.

One day my friends were talking about a new boy that came to my school and didn't talk at all. They called him a bum, jerk and other bad names, but I stood up for him anyway and said, "You don't know him to judge him. You wouldn't want people picking on you, especially if you were new like him." That took courage for me because it was some of my friends and they didn't want to be my friend because I stood up for someone that was not cool.

After this, my ex-friends gave me the silent treatment. Every time they would be captains for football they would never pick me, and we used to be the bomb squad. They also stopped calling me on the weekends to make plans to go to the movies and other things. I hated that because I missed them and we always used to go out together.

A few days later I watched them play football, hoping they would let me play. I was thinking that I regretted sticking up for that stupid little boy. A teacher came up to me, tapping my head, smiling and told me it was a good thing I did. That made me remember that what I did was courageous and I felt good again. All in all, it feels good to help people and to stand up for something that you think is right.

The Courage of Boston's Children, Volume XII, The Max Warburg Courage Curriculum and the Boston Public Schools, Houghton Mifflin Company, 2003.

1. Can you imagine sticking up for someone who was bullied if it meant losing your friends? Explain your answer.

_____

_____

_____

_____

2. What can you do if you don't like to bully people but your friends do?

_____

_____

_____

_____

3. If you want to make new friends what can you do?

_____

_____

_____

_____

4. Are there any other ways Wilnord could have helped the new boy?

_____

_____

_____

_____

5. Answer question a or b.
   a. Have you silently watched bullying? Without using real names describe what happened and how you felt.

_____

_____

_____

_____

_____

_____

_____

_____

b. Describe a character in a book or someone you saw in a TV show, movie, or video game that silently watched another person be bullied.

• Name of character_____

• Title of book, TV show, movie or video _____

_____

_____

_____

_____

_____

_____

_____

6. If you were a student at Parker Elementary School and saw Avery bullied, do you think you would speak up for him or ask an adult to help? Why or why not?

_____

_____

_____

_____

_____

_____

_____

_____

_____

RESPECT AGREEMENT MEETING

Meet with the person or persons who you made a *Respect Agreement* with. List examples of how you treat each other with respect. List examples, if any, of how you treat each other with disrespect. List ideas of how you can help each other succeed in following your agreement.

1. Ways you treat each other with respect.

_____
_____
_____
_____
_____
_____

2. Ways you treat each other with disrespect.

_____
_____
_____
_____
_____
_____

3. How can you help each other succeed in following your agreement?

_____
_____
_____
_____
_____
_____

SIX

Who Are the Helpers?

Objectives

- To provide students with a wide variety of illustrations of how they can assertively stick up for themselves when treated with disrespect.

- To explore the concept of bullying.

- To identify the characteristics of *helpers*.

- To introduce the concept of sticking up for others and the powerful role helpers play in stopping bullying at school.

- To help students develop assertive communication skills.

- To explore ways students can help stop bullying at school.

Chapter Summary, *Avery Quinn: Eye of the Storm*

Avery's father learns about the bullying and how Mr. Sergio is helping his son. Finally the two adults work as a team. The father plans to involve the Principal as well. Mr. Sergio teaches Avery more assertiveness strategies which Avery's father reinforces at home.

Suggestions for Success

The focused topic in this section, *Who Are the Helpers?*, teaches children a variety of ways to help students who are bullied. Since the core objective of this curriculum is to help the silent majority become more of a helping majority, this focused topic is very important to include.

Activities

Avery Quinn: Eye of the Storm

    a. Read aloud to the class *Avery Quinn: Eye of the Storm*.

    b. Use the Chapter Discussion questions to stimulate conversation about the chapter.

Select from the recommended activities below, especially those in bold.

1. Role-play: Agree #1

This is a whole class activity, which could also be done in pairs.

    a. Distribute the Handout: *Agree #1* to each student.

    b. Assign a child to read aloud the story of the athletic child and the chubby child.

    c. Ask volunteers to role-play the story for the class, using the script provided.

    d. De-brief. Call volunteers by their true names. Ask them how it felt to read the parts of the characters they played.

2. Role-play: Agree #2

    a. Distribute the Handout: *Agree #2* to each student.

    b. Assign a child to read the fictional story of Jake and Link.

    c. Ask volunteers to role-play the story, using the script provided.

    d. De-brief. Call volunteers by their true names. Ask them how it felt to read the parts of the characters they played.

3. Who Are the Helpers?

    a. Distribute the Handout: *Who Are the Helpers?* for students to individually read and complete.

    b. Read aloud the questions on the handout. Ask students to share their answers. After the discussion, students turn in their completed work.

4. Thomas and Lakiesha—students who bullied others and then became *helpers.*

    a. Give students a handout of *Thomas* or *Lakiesha* to read.

    b. Discuss the handouts by asking students to describe:

      • the students who were bullied,

      • Thomas or Lakiesha's behavior when (s)he was involved in bullying, and

      • Thomas or Lakiesha's behavior when (s)he was a helper.

6. Journal

Students respond to the following question in their journals.

    a. What can adults do to help children who are bullied?

Avery Quinn: *Eye of the Storm*

That night my Dad saw me practicing bully blocking skills in front of my bedroom mirror. He looked worried. I told him about being picked on and that Mr. Sergio was showing me how to stick up for myself.

Dad abruptly sat down on the edge of my bed. His head sunk into his hands. His body shook a little. I held my breath.

After awhile Dad stood up and gave me a big hug. He wasn't shaking anymore.

"I haven't been protecting you," he said.

"It's not your fault Dad."

"How did Mr. Sergio know?" he asked.

"He saw stuff. Same thing happened to him when he was a kid," I said.

Dad looked at me but didn't say anything.

"Can you help me too?"

"Of course. I'll call the Principal."

I didn't want him to. I pleaded, "Just talk to Mr. Sergio."

In the morning my father drove me to school. It was so early that no students were outside. Dad went in the office. I took my time walking down the empty hall toward my classroom.

"Did you talk to my Dad?" I asked at recess.

"Yeah," said Mr. Sergio.

"What are you going to do?"

"It was nice meeting him. I'm glad you told him."

"What are you going to do?" I repeated.

"I guess he's planning on giving you rides to and from school."

"Don't you think that's too much for him?"

"It's what he wants to do," said Mr. Sergio.

There was a moment when neither of us spoke.

"I did the Stone Wall thing," I said.

"And?"

"It went kind of good."

"You're doing great Avery."

I nodded.

Mr. Sergio stood perfectly still. Since he usually was in constant motion it was strange to see him not moving at all. "Interested in being as calm as the eye of a hurricane?" he asked.

I shrugged my shoulders.

"Become an *actor*. When the kids say something mean, pretend you can't hear them. Give them a surprising answer like agreeing with what they say. Gently change the subject, shrug your shoulders, or tell a joke."

Being an actor will be hard work, I thought. *But I was calm after I stonewalled the guys. Maybe I'm half way there.* "How many bully blocking skills are left?" I asked.

"Two," said Mr. Sergio. "Call the kids who pick on you by their real names; ask adults and friends for help. Some adults are more supportive than others are. If you tell adults and they don't help, keep telling until you find ones that will."

I nodded.

"How can you get yourself some friends?" he asked.

"I don't know," I confessed.

"How about the boy who smiled at you?"

"What do I do?"

"Talk to him," said Mr. Sergio.

"About?"

"Anything."

"Anything?"

"Natural disasters?"

"I don't think I'll get a chance."

"With all the strengths you have, Avery, I am sure you'll find a way."

"Strengths?"

"Yes. You're great to talk to, smart, fun to be with, a hard worker, and brave."

I was used to feeling ashamed for being weak. It was strange to hear myself described that way.

"Thanks," I said.

"And one more thing. Use your imagination. Successful athletes use a technique called *Visualization* to help them improve their game. Before matches, tennis players visualize exactly how they will stand and hold their rackets."

Mr. Sergio pretended to hold a tennis racket.

"They imagine how they will hit the ball," he said, pretending to hit a tennis ball with his invisible racket. "They see themselves playing well and feeling great. Try it. Shut your eyes. Imagine that some kids are bothering you, but you stand tall and feel okay."

He paused. "Can you see it?"

"Um," I said, opening my eyes.

"Shut your eyes. Try again," instructed Mr. Sergio. "See yourself next to Ryon. Your shoulders are back, your head high. You take a deep breath, stay calm, and speak strongly." He paused again. "Got it?"

"Sort of. Maybe," I said.

"Can you imagine yourself flying into and out of a hurricane," continued Mr. Sergio, "and feeling great afterwards?"

I smiled. He threw me a red and white striped Frisbee. We played catch for awhile.

Mr. Sergio asked, "Before the bell rings, what can I learn?"

"There are about a million earthquakes every year," I told him. "Sometimes they last only seconds. Most tsunamis are caused by them."

"Good luck with being an actor," said Mr.

Sergio. "Give the earth and waters a little rumble."

"I'm going to be an actor," I told my Dad when he picked me up.

"An actor?"

"Actors surprise jerks by agreeing with them. They pretend they don't hear mean words. They do stuff like start talking about something totally different. They act like comedians and tell jokes."

Instead of going straight home, Dad stopped by Quinn's Books. "I'm going to the attic," he said, "be right back." I slid down in the front seat with my feet on the dashboard and thought about my favorite actors. Dad returned with a stack of books. "Maybe these will help," he said, dumping them in my lap. "I enjoyed them when I was your age."

I looked at the titles. They were joke books. I opened one and read, "Why are fish smart?"

"Because they live in schools," said Dad.

I read another.

"What kind of hair do oceans have?"

"Wavy," answered Dad.

"Knock, knock."

"Who's there?"

"Wooden," I said.

Dad jumped to the punch line. "Wooden you like to know?"

It turned out he had memorized the answers to all the jokes in the books.

That night, after I crawled into bed, Dad gave me another hug and said, "Good luck being a funny actor."

Chapter Discussion

Discuss *Avery Quinn: Eye of the Storm*. Ask students not to use children's real names during this conversation. Advise them to communicate privately later if they need to.

1. What does it mean to stick up for yourself by being an *actor*?

2. Raise your hand if you have ever used a *Visualization* technique to help yourself do something well. Describe your experiences. (If no one has an example, describe one from your own life.)

Empowering Children to Help Stop Bullying at School

AGREE #1

This activity is based on a true story. It requires three people.

Two athletic-looking fifth graders stand outside the school gym. A chubby fourth grader walks past them. The fifth graders point and laugh at the chubby boy. One of them says, "Don't even think of trying out for the basketball team. Go on a diet. That's the sport for you."

The chubby boy closes his eyes for a second and takes a deep breath. He looks at the fifth graders and calmly says, "I like basketball but I'm not that good. I'm a super sports commentator though. You should check me out on You Tube. I get a lot of hits."

The chubby boy takes another deep breath and says, "You guys are fantastic B-ball players. I wish I was as good as you."

The other fifth grader, surprised by the younger boy's response says, "If you want, we could teach you some of our moves."

"Sure," says the fourth grader. The three boys walk together into the gym.

1. Role-play the parts of two fifth graders, and a fourth grader who assertively speaks up for himself.

Two fifth graders

Stage directions: Act unfriendly. Point and laugh at the fourth grader. One of you say...
Don't even think of playing basketball. Go on a diet. That's the sport for you.

A fourth grader

Stage directions: Close your eyes for a moment. Take a deep breath. Look at the fifth graders. Speak calmly. Say...
I like basketball but I'm not that good. I'm a super sports commentator though. You should check me out on You Tube. I get a lot of hits.

Stage directions: Take another deep breath.
You guys are fantastic B-ball players. I wish I was as good as you.

Two fifth graders

Stage directions: Look surprised and friendly. The person who didn't speak before says...
If you want, we could teach you some of our moves.

A fourth grader

Stage directions: Smile and say...
Sure.

Two fifth graders and a fourth grader

Stage directions: Walk together. Pretend you are going into the gym.

2. Choose a different role to play. Do the role-play again as a different character.

3. After completing this skit, de-brief. Call each other by your real names. Ask each other...
   a. What did it feel like to play the part of one of the fifth graders?
   b. What did it feel like to play the part of the fourth grader?

AGREE #2

An example of agreeing with someone who is disrespectful is in the book, *Jake Drake, Bully Buster* by Andrew Clements. When the fictional character, Link Baxter, calls Jake Drake "Jake Flake," Jake Drake acts cool and agrees with Link by saying, "Yeah, that's a good one! Or how about Snake Drake? Or Cheesecake Drake? Or maybe Shaky Jake? Yeah, Shaky Jake."

This activity is for two people. Take turns pretending to be Link and Jake.

Link Baxter: Jake Flake

Jake Drake: Yeah, that's a good one! Or how about Snake Drake? Or Cheesecake Drake? Or maybe Shaky Jake. Yeah, Shaky Jake.

After completing this skit, de-brief. Ask each other...
- What did it feel like to read the disrespectful statements?
- What did it feel like to read the assertive statements?

WHO ARE THE HELPERS?

Mr. Sergio, the bus driver, the boy who gives Avery a *thumbs-up* sign and the students who yell, "Stop, Ryon, Stop," are helpers. Helpers can be children or adults. It takes confidence and courage for children to be helpers. Just one young person on the side of another who is bullied can be enough for a child who is bullying to back off.

Maddie, in the book *The Hundred Dresses*, decided that she never wanted to be a silent witness again. She vowed that in the future she would speak up for someone who is treated mean. She would say nice things to the one who is bullied, act friendly and stick up for her or him.

Zinkoff's family and neighbors, in the book *Loser*, help him by doing fun things with Zinkoff and liking him for who he is.

A girl in the book *In the Year of the Boar and Jackie Robinson*, helps Shirley Temple Wong when she is excluded from playing baseball, by saying, "Who says my friend Shirley here can't play?"

In the book *Attack of the Killer Fishsticks*, fifth graders, Dave, Jennifer, Johnny and Liz stick up for Max, a new student at their school who wears a tie and is bullied. They also invite Max to join their Wacky Facts Lunch Bunch club.

Helpers are leaders of kindness. They:
- ask adults for help,
- ask or tell children who bully to stop,
- listen and talk to children who are bullied,
- say nice things about someone who is bullied,
- sit/stand next to, or walk with children who are bullied,
- tell their friends how they feel when their friends act mean, and
- invite children who are bullied to do something fun, join a game or group activity.

1. Describe a situation where someone at school helped a person who was treated disrespectfully. If you saw this happen, re-tell the story without using real names. If you have not seen this happen, make up a story where someone at school helps a student who is treated with disrespect.

_____

_____

_____

_____

_____

_____

_____

_____

_____

_____

_____

_____

2. Choose a character that you read about in a book, or saw in a TV show, movie, or video game that helped someone who was treated with disrespect.

   a. Name of the character. _____

   b. Title of the book, TV show, movie, or video game. _____
   _____

3. Which of the following did the helper do? Check the correct ones.

   _____ asked an adult for help

   _____ asked or told children who bullied to stop

   _____ listened and talked to a child who was bullied

   _____ said nice things about someone who was bullied

   _____ sat/stood next to, or walked with a child who was bullied

   _____ told her or his friends how (s)he felt when they acted mean

   _____ invited a child who was bullied to do something fun, join a game or group activity

4. Write a summary of the story describing who was treated with disrespect, the behavior of those acting disrespectful, and the behavior of the helper.

   _____
   _____
   _____
   _____
   _____
   _____
   _____
   _____
   _____
   _____
   _____
   _____
   _____
   _____
   _____
   _____
   _____
   _____
   _____
   _____

THOMAS

Courage in my life

 I admit it. I was a bully. You name it I've done it. I've called kids names, made fun of kids' weight, made kids cry of embarrassment and many other terrible things you can imagine. Ever since the first grade, I've always been the tallest kid in the class. I used that size as an advantage. I hung out with all the troublemakers in the class, just trying to fit in.

 During all of this I never took into consideration that I was hurting someone else's feelings. I was with the "cool kids" and that was all that mattered to me. Each day the gang and I would randomly select our new victim.

 This one kid that comes to mind is "Will." Will was a little overweight and was not popular. He was smart, always did his homework, and never bothered anybody. This was Will's unlucky week in the third grade. I continued to do this for a long time. Taunting and teasing this "good kid" was becoming an everyday occurrence. This whole time I was hurting Will's feelings more and more each day, never thinking about how he felt or how it may affect him. ...

 Then one day one of my so called "friends" called Will a nasty name referring to his weight. Watching the look on Will's face was "this had gone too far." For once during my life I felt bad for someone else. I didn't like the way it made me feel. I proceeded to tell the other bullies that this had gone way too far. I told them that what they had done has hurt him really bad. The biggest troublemaker in the group told me to mind my own business. Instead of saying something back to this kid and getting into a fight, I walked over to Will and apologized for what I'd done in the past to him. I think at first Will didn't believe me. The look on his face said "please do not hurt me again." But slowly the sadness in his eyes disappeared. Then Will and I became great friends. Whenever someone tried to tease him, I would be there to help have his back. I am now at a new school, and I do not get to see Will anymore.

 It's a lot easier to join the cool crowd and make fun of people just to belong. I showed courage when I stood up for Will. People like Will have to show courage every day. If more people stood up for the Wills in this world, this world would be a better place. I know this isn't as courageous as jumping into a fire to save someone, but it made me feel just as courageous.

The Courage of Boston's Children, Volume XIV, The Max Warburg Courage Curriculum, Inc. and the Boston Public Schools, Houghton Mifflin Company, 2005.

LAKIESHA

Courage in My Life

A time when I showed courage is when I stood up for something and someone even though all my friends looked at me differently afterwards. I mean who really cares about what others think about you? As long as you did the right thing, it shouldn't matter what other people say. The reason I'm saying this is because the beginning of sixth grade started just like fourth and fifth grades. It started with the same boy who always got picked on. And I will admit that I picked on him, too.

One day I realized that the only reason I picked on him was because I wanted to fit in. Everyone else picked on him, so I figured that in order to fit in I had to pick on him as well. And I did, until I got to the sixth grade.

One day during lunch, we were all sitting at a lunch table. We had already recycled our trays and used the bathroom. We were waiting for our next specialist to pick us up. That was when I noticed everyone screaming and running away from this boy. They did this just to make him feel bad.

I went over there and told them, "Stop teasing and treating him like he's going to bite you." But they all just looked at me like I was kidding, and they kept teasing him.

I got so angry that I brought up the problem in class meeting. When I did, I told the boy, "The only reason I disrespected you was to fit in. But then I realized that if I had to treat you like trash to have friends, I guess I don't need any."

It's not like people treated him any differently after I apologized to him. I explained to everyone that if you treat people like that, it just means that you are jealous, insecure, or just plain evil.

The Courage of Boston's Children, Volume XIV, The Max Warburg Courage Curriculum, Inc. and the Boston Public Schools, Houghton Mifflin Company, 2005.

SEVEN

Tragedy & Courage

Chapter Summary, *Avery Quinn: Making Waves*

The morning and afternoon bullying is temporarily stopped because Avery's father drives him back and forth to school. Avery's desire to make a friend is greater than his wish to escape the bullying. So he convinces his father to let him ride the bus again because that is where a boy who smiled at him is. This time Avery deals with the bullying with more confidence and skill. Simultaneously some students who previously joined in or silently watched Avery being bullied stick up for him instead.

Suggestion for Success

1. The *Courage in My Life* essay activity in this section is one of the two most significant exercises in this book. The Handout: *Nelson* activity in section Eight is the other. The essays in this section provide peer *helper* stories that are very important for children to be introduced to. Essays that you don't need for this activity should be utilized as part of the *Books, Stories, and Essays on Bullying* activity in section Ten.

2. During the Visualization exercise, if students are having difficulty keeping their eyes closed, you can motion for them to do so, but don't speak to them, or let it distract you from reading the Visualization as it is described.

Activities

Avery Quinn: Making Waves
   a. Read *Avery Quinn: Making Waves* aloud to the class.
   b. Use the Chapter Discussion questions to stimulate conversation about the chapter.

Most of the activities in this section are highly recommended.

Objectives

- To explore the concept of bullying.

- To provide information on the seriousness of bullying.

- To explore the concepts of sticking up for yourself and others.

- To provide students with a wide variety of illustrations of how they can assertively stick up for themselves when treated with disrespect.

- To help students develop assertive communication skills.

- To explore how children and adults can work together to stop bullying at school.

1. Tragedy
   a. Read aloud *Tragedy*.
   b. Use the Chapter Discussion questions to stimulate conversation about bullying tragedies.

2. Courage
   a. Arrange the class in a circle.
   b. Give each student a copy of the Handout: *Courage*.
   c. Go around the circle, with each student reading one line of the song.
   d. Use the Courage Discussion questions to stimulate conversation about the song.

3. Courage in My Life

   Sixth graders from the Boston Public Schools in Boston, MA wrote the following *Courage in My Life* essays. Each essay is summarized below.

   Troy: In third grade spoke up for a girl who was bullied

   Amy: In second grade asked an unpopular girl to sit with her at lunch

   Lauren: In fourth grade told her friends that she wouldn't join them in games if a girl who was excluded couldn't play too

   Slater: In fifth grade spoke up for a friend who was bullied by another friend

   Guivens: In K–2 spoke up for a friend who was bullied

   Christina: In third grade spoke up for a group of "special needs children" who were treated with disrespect

   Holly: In third grade befriended a boy who was bullied

   Latoya: In sixth grade saw a classmate bullied and reported it to a teacher

   Crystal: On an end-of-the year trip, fifth graders went to a dance at a hotel. Crystal's friends made fun of a physically challenged boy who was dancing by himself. Crystal chose to befriend and stand up for the boy instead.

   These are two more examples of helpers:

   Todd: Reported the situation to his father/coach. Told his friends how he felt when they were disrespectful to a new boy on their team.

   Marissa: Classmates calmly told a child who was teasing Marissa to stop. They helped her report the incident to their classroom teacher and sat with her until the bullying stopped.

a. Divide the class into groups.

b. Give each group one *Courage in My Life* story to:
- read,
- answer the handout questions,
- create a visual, and
- prepare to re-tell the story by including a description of the person who was treated with disrespect, the behavior of those who were acting disrespectfully, and the actions of the helper.

c. Reconvene. Each group tells the *Courage in My Life* story that they read.

d. Each group answers questions from the rest of the class.

4. Visualization

Do this Visualization before the role-play *Speak Up for Others*.
In (parentheses) are instructions for the teacher. In *italics* are what you say to your class.

Close your eyes. Take three slow, deep breaths.
   (Pause. Take three slow, deep breaths.)
Imagine you see one student at school treating another student with disrespect.
   (Pause. Take a slow, deep breath in and out.)
You stay calm, pull your shoulders back, and stand tall.
   (Pause. Take another slow, deep breath in and out.)
Hold your head high. Use assertive words to speak up for the student who is bullied.
   (Pause. Take a slow, deep breath in and out.)
You remain calm and walk away with the student who was treated with disrespect.
   (Pause. Take two slow, deep breaths in and out.)
When you are ready, open your eyes.
   (Pause until students have opened their eyes.)
Stand up and shake out your arms.

5. **Role-play: Speak Up for Others #1**

Involve either pairs or the whole class in role-plays. Use approach a or b.

a. Divide students into pairs. Give each pair a copy of *Speak Up for Others #1*. Explain that:
- One student will read the disrespectful statements and the other pretend to stick up for Avery.
- Everyone speaking as Avery should stand tall, pull their shoulders back, hold their heads high, take a slow, deep, breath and speak calmly without yelling.

- After students complete the role-play once, they switch places. The one who played Avery first now reads the disrespectful statement and vice versa.
- De-brief. Children call each other by their real names and ask each other how it felt to read the disrespectful and assertive statements.

b. A simpler approach, and if the group needs more structure, is for the teacher to read the disrespectful statements and one at a time, or the whole group together, gives the assertive responses. Then de-brief. Call children by their real names. Ask them how it felt to say the assertive responses.

6. Homework: Speak Up for Others #2

a. Give each student copies of the Handouts: *Speak Up for Others #1* and *2*.

b. Children repeat the *Speak Up for Others #1* activity at home with a family member, friend, neighbor, or teacher and complete the *Speak Up for Others #2* handout.

c. As a follow-up to the homework, ask the class if they were students at Parker Elementary School and wanted to help Avery, what would they do?

7. Journal

Students respond to the following questions in their journals.

a. Write an answer to one of the questions below.

- Have you helped someone who was bullied? Is so, what did you do? How did you feel?
- Have you helped someone who was treated with disrespect? If so, what did you do? How did you feel?
- In what ways did Troy, Amy, Lauren, Slater, Guivens, Christina, Holly, Latoya, Todd or Marissa's classmates help someone who was treated with disrespect?

Avery Quinn: *Making Waves*

My father brought me to school early again. At recess, after our warm-up, Mr. Sergio and I made up plays about surprising and agreeing with children who bully, changing the subject, and pretending not to hear what they say. At the end of the day Dad purposely picked me up late. I waited in the front office until he arrived. Then he drove me to the public library so I could get more joke books.

On the ride home I opened one and read, "Knock, knock."

"Who's there?" answered Dad.

"Avenue."

"Avenue who?"

"Avenue heard this joke before?"

He hadn't.

I tried another, "Why do seagulls live near the sea?"

Dad shook his head.

"If they lived near the bay, they would be called bagels."

He laughed.

"What happens when you throw a green stone in the Red Sea?"

He didn't know.

"It gets wet," I said grinning.

We went through a whole book. I stumped my father every time.

For the next two weeks he drove me to and from school. Both at recess and at home I practiced speaking up for myself like an actor would. But mostly I thought about the boy who had smiled at me and told myself, *he could be my friend.*

"I don't want to ride with you anymore," I told Dad. "On Wednesday I'm taking the bus."

"I don't think so," he replied.

"Ryon's the one who shouldn't be on the bus," I argued, "not me."

"I'll tell the Principal to take him off."

"Don't make things worse Dad."

"Letting Mrs. Shane know what's going on will make things better, not worse. I can't chance you getting hurt."

"Let me see if this acting stuff works," I told him. "Could you ask Mr. Sergio what he thinks?" I crossed my fingers, even though doing so hadn't worked before.

On Wednesday morning the air was chilly. I shoved both of my hands into my jacket pockets. I noticed that most of the red, orange and yellow leaves had fallen to the ground. After talking to Mr. Sergio Dad decided he'd wait about a week and then call Mrs. Shane.

As soon as the bus arrived I regretted my decision. Ryon, wearing a purple and white soccer uniform, was sitting on the aisle side of the front seat where I usually sat. I wasn't sure what to do. There was no other empty seat. I stepped toward the window side of the seat and told myself, *do what you've practiced.*

I pointed out the window, "Ryon, look at that airplane. It's right on time. Air France I believe."

"You're lame," said Ryon.

I pretended he didn't make me nervous. "Thanks for the compliment," I said and sat down.

Some students laughed.

"I'm out of here," exclaimed Ryon. He jumped up and bolted down the aisle.

I looked behind me. Many rows away was the boy I wanted for a friend. He waved. I waited for him to get off the bus. But Carlos got to me first.

His happy look had returned. "Aberry Quince is back," he said to his pack of girls.

I asked myself, *what would Robin Williams say?* "Carlos," I said, "if you think I'm strange you should see my goat."

Carlos stepped in front of me, looking less friendly than seconds before. "Limp leg," he said.

I shrugged my shoulders and said, "I guess I've got the limpest leg around." It felt like I was driving a motor boat through choppy waves.

"Way to go, Avery," said one of the fifth grade girls. With her curly brown hair and blue eyes she looked a lot like my Dad and me.

"Why are you sticking up for *him*?" Carlos asked the girl.

Yes, I shouted inside my head.

The two of them argued while I went on my way. When I got to the west wing of the first floor, in the doorway of the other fourth grade classroom, was the boy I had waited for. *He must have passed by me when I got stopped by Carlos*, I thought. *Was he waiting for me?*

Enzo blocked my view. He cried, "My leg, my leg, I need a new leg."

I used a joke from one of my father's books. "What runs, Enzo, but never walks?"

"Not you," he said.

The teacher in the other classroom told her students to go inside. She was shutting the door.

"Want to race down the hall? teased Marcella.

Enzo and the other boy were inside their classroom now.

"Water runs, Marcella, never walks," I said, waving goodbye.

At recess I told Mr. Sergio about my morning, "You're cookin', Avery, a born actor."

"Acting works the best," I said.

He handed me a hockey stick and used another to pass me a ball made from crumpled newspaper wrapped in masking tape.

"All of the bully blocking skills are good ones. In the beginning, you can't tell if they are working, but each lays a foundation for the rest. They build upon each other, until you reach the sky." He pointed at the ceiling of the gym.

I'll reach the sky, I thought, *when I learn to fly*.

For the rest of recess we played hockey with the newspaper ball.

After school, I was the last one on the bus. I didn't see my friend. Ryon was in the second row, right behind where I sat. He greeted me with, "If it isn't little lonely."

It wasn't true. I didn't feel lonely anymore. "Thanks," I said.

"Daddy's been keeping you in the cradle?" he asked.

I thought, *if only I was Robin Williams*.

"Daddy's little baby girl."

"Knock it off," I said.

Ryon was so close to my face I could smell his breath. "Hiding behind your Daddy, baby girl?"

"Knock it off."

"Scared little girly boy?"

Ryon kept repeating himself. I tried to think of something funny to say.

"Off it knock. It off knock. Off knock it. It knock off."

I got more laughs. Somebody even clapped.

Chapter Discussion

Discuss *Avery Quinn: Making Waves*. Ask students not to use children's real names during this conversation. Advise them to communicate privately later if they need to.

1. How are the characters in the story changing?

2. How is Avery being helped?

3. What will it take for Ryon, Carlos, Enzo and Marcella to stop bullying Avery?

Reading: Tragedy

Every day researchers learn something about bullying. Studies done in the United States conclude that one or two of every ten students at school are bullied. In a school of a hundred students then, ten to twenty students might be bullied.

Bathrooms, locker rooms, play fields, halls, classrooms and lunchrooms. That's where bullying in school happens the most. Buses, bus stops, vacant lots, empty buildings and fields, walking and biking routes to and from school, public swimming pools, movie theaters, homes, parties, summer camps, over the phone, and on the Internet. That's where it happens the most outside of school.

Too often students who are bullied don't tell adults. Maybe they feel ashamed, don't want to be called a *tattletale, snitch, rat, fink,* or *squealer* or are afraid that if they tell adults, the problem will get worse.

Bullying can be much more severe than what Avery is experiencing. Some students are seriously bullied for a long time, and become so hopeless they want to kill themselves. This is especially true for children who are not popular and picked on by a group of students, with no one sticking up for them. Some youth become so full of rage and revenge they want to kill other people as well as themselves. Seventy-one percent of *school shooters* felt that, before they became violent, they had been targets of severe and longstanding threats, attacks, injury, persecution, and bullying.

Discussion: Tragedy

Discuss *Tragedy*. Ask students to refrain from using children's real names during this conversation. Advise them to communicate privately later if they need to.

1. Ask students to raise their hand if they think
   a. the cafeteria in our school is a place where children get bullied
   b. the playground at our school is a place where students get bullied
   c. children at our school are bullied in bathrooms
   d. children at our school are bullied in the hallways
   e. students at our school are bullied on the school buses
   f. students at our school have been bullied over the Internet
   g. students at our school have been bullied through text messaging

2. Have you heard, read about, or seen on the news/in a movie/video game or TV show, someone who was bullied who killed themselves and/or other people?

3. How can bullying at school and tragedies related to bullying be prevented?

COURAGE

A small thing once happened at school
That brought up a question for me.
And somehow, it forced me to see
The price that I pay to be cool.
Diane is a girl that I know.
She's strange, like she doesn't belong.
I don't mean to say that that's wrong.
We don't like to be with her, though.
And so, when we all made a plan
To have this big party at Sue's,
Most kids in the school got the news,
But no one invited Diane.

The thing about Taft Junior High,
Is, secrets don't last very long.
I acted like nothing was wrong
When I saw Diane start to cry.
I know you may think that I'm cruel.
It doesn't make me very proud.
I just went along with the crowd.
It's sad, but you have to at school.
You can't pick the friends you prefer.
You fit in as well as you can.
I couldn't be friends with Diane,
'Cause then they would treat me like her.

In one class at Taft Junior High,
We study what people have done
With gas chamber, bomber, and gun
In Auschwitz, Japan, and My Lai.
I don't understand all I learn.
Sometimes I just sit there and cry.
The whole world stood idly by
To watch as the innocent burned.
Like robots obeying some rule.
Atrocities done by the mob.
All innocent, doing their job.
And what was it for? Was it cool?

The world was aware of this hell,
But how many cried out in shame?
What heroes, and who was to blame?
A story that no one dared tell.
I promise to do what I can.
To not let it happen again.
To care for all women and men.
I'll start by inviting Diane.

from *Starting Small: Songs for Growing People* by Bob Blue

Discussion: Courage

1. What does it mean to be someone who is strange and doesn't belong?

2. What does the speaker in the *Courage* song mean by:

   a. The price that I pay to be cool.

   b. I just went along with the crowd.
      It's sad, but you have to at school.
      You can't pick the friends you prefer.
      You fit in as well as you can.

   c. I couldn't be friends with Diane
      'Cause then they would treat me like her.

3. How is Diane being treated?

4. Do you think she was intentionally excluded from activities involving students who are more popular than her?

5. Do you think the person speaking in this song decides to care about how Diane feels about being left out?

6. Why does the person speaking decide to invite Diane to Sue's party?

7. Why is the song titled *Courage*?

TROY

Courage in My Life

Hi, my name is Troy Williams and this is how my story started. Three years ago I was in third grade, and during the middle of the school year I showed courage by standing up for a classmate. There was this girl in my class and every day people made fun of her clothing and shoes because they were dirty. Her dress had holes in it and her shirt had stains on it.

She had some friends, but they weren't real friends because they made fun of her, too. I did not like what they were saying about her even though I did not know her that well because we did not speak to each other. One day she came to school with the same clothes she'd had on the day before, and everybody started to make fun of her. She started to cry, so I got up and said, "Why do you make fun of her? What has she ever done to you? I believe you should treat people how you want to be treated." They all stopped and listened to me, and after that, they stopped making fun of her. It took a lot of courage to stand up to my class, but I did it.

The Courage of Boston's Children, Volume XVII, The Max Warburg Courage Curriculum, Inc. and the Boston Public Schools, Northeastern University, 2008.

1. Describe the student who was bullied.

_____

_____

_____

2. Describe the behavior of those who were bullying.

_____

_____

_____

3. Describe how Troy helped the girl who was bullied.

_____

_____

_____

4. On a separate piece of paper draw a picture to show how Troy helped his classmate.

5. Prepare to tell the story of how Troy helped a classmate who was bullied. Include in your storytelling, a description of the person who was treated with disrespect, the behavior of those who were disrespectful, and Troy's actions.

6. Tell Troy's story to your class and possibly other audiences.

AMY

Courage in My Life

In second grade there was a girl named Alycia that no one wanted to go near. She was quiet and looked kind of weird. She had thick glasses and wore braces, which made her look like a bug. I didn't really notice her that much. I kept hearing people talk about how she looked and acted. Then a lot of kids started teasing her and imitating her. I wanted to help her, but I had to go along with my crew. They didn't like her.

Then one day I did the most courageous thing I could have done. I asked Alycia if she wanted to sit next to me at lunch. I don't know what came over me. During lunch my friends hardly talked to me and some kids were staring and whispering. I felt kind of embarrassed, but I talked to her and then days later other kids were too. It turned out she wasn't that weird person that everybody thought she was. A lot of kids befriended her and she finally smiled.

That time I felt like a hero. It was like I made a difference in somebody's life. All it took was a little courage. It was inside of me all the time. Courage is found within us all, just waiting to come out.

The Courage of Boston's Children, Volume III, The Max Warburg Courage Curriculum, Inc. and the Boston Public Schools, Houghton Mifflin Company, 1994.

1. Describe the behavior of the student who was bullied.

_____

_____

_____

2. Describe the behavior of those who were bullying.

_____

_____

_____

3. Describe how Amy helped the student who was bullied.

_____

_____

_____

4. On a separate piece of paper draw a picture to show how Amy helped Alycia.

5. Prepare to tell the story of how Amy helped a student who was bullied. Include In your storytelling, a description of the person who was treated with disrespect, the behavior of those who were disrespectful, and Amy's actions.

6. Tell Amy's story to your class and possibly other audiences.

LAUREN

Courage in My Life

Courage, to me, is the ability to defend a person's own beliefs and opinions, especially those who are not able or strong enough to do so themselves. Courage was just a word I read about in papers and books. I really never knew the true meaning of it until I was in the fourth grade. We had a new girl in our class. Her name was Vivian, and she had just come to America from China about a year before. She spoke limited English, and she was very shy. I think she was uncomfortable in her new country. Every day I would say, "Hi, Vivian," and she eventually would say, "Hi" back to me. I had a hard time trying to understand why the girls did not say hello to her or invite her to play in games at recess and lunch time.

One day I thought to myself, "This is not fair. It's mean, hurtful, and this behavior is not typical of all people." As I lay on my bed, thinking about Vivian, I said to myself, "I am going to do something to change this, even if it means losing some of my friends." The next morning I went to school, and proudly announced that I didn't want to play in anyone's games unless Vivian was included. I must tell you that I too am a little shy, and this was a little out of my style as far as my classmates were concerned. They were a little shocked, but they soon learned that I was serious and meant what I said. It took a couple of days before they invited Vivian and me to join them in all the classroom activities.

Truthfully, I never thought that I had the ability, fearlessness, and courage to speak up for someone who was alone in a strange classroom. I would do it again. Vivian did become part of our classroom scene, and she and I became good friends. Sometimes you have to give a little effort, have a little courage, and spread a little friendship to make the world a better place.

The Courage of Boston's Children, Volume XV, The Max Warburg Courage Curriculum, Inc. and the Boston Public Schools, Houghton Mifflin Company, 2006.

1. Describe the student who was bullied.

_____

_____

_____

2. Describe the behavior of those who were bullying.

_____

_____

_____

3. Describe how Lauren helped the student who was bullied.

_____

_____

_____

4. On a separate piece of paper draw a picture to show how Lauren helped Vivian.

5. Prepare to tell the story of how Lauren helped Vivian. Include in your storytelling, a description of the person who was treated with disrespect, the behavior of those who were disrespectful, and Lauren's actions.

6. Tell Lauren's story to your class and possibly other audiences.

SLATER

Courage in My Life

Courage comes in many different ways. It can come from being sad, mad, nervous or scared. But when I was courageous, it was kind of funny. Well, it happened one day when I came home from school. This is how it began:

"How was school today?" my mom asked.

"Bad," I replied. "Mom, I have to tell you something," I told her.

"What, honey?" my mom asked. I know my mom was trying to be nice, but sometimes she can get kind of annoying.

"Please don't call me 'honey.' I'm in fifth grade. Anyway, my friend Eddy is being bullied. But the problem is it's not just a bully—the bully is one of my best friends, Billy!" I exclaimed.

My mom started to look worried; I expected this, because my mom gets worried even about the smallest things.

"It is getting pretty bad. He has said some of the most hurtful things I could ever imagine," I said.

My mom looked even more worried.

"What in the world should I do?" I asked, full of dread.

"You can't just ignore him; you've got to do something, like tell him to stop," my mom said, trying to give me advice.

After I had a snack, I started to head upstairs when, "BRING, BRING," the phone rang.

"I'll get it," I told my mom. I picked up the phone.

"Hello," I said into the phone.

"Hi, it's me, Eddy," Eddy said. He sounded as if he was quivering. Eddy was a very sensitive person. He wasn't the type of person to stand up to a bully and tell him to stop.

"What should I do about the bully? I'm nervous about tomorrow at school," Eddy said.

I explained what we had to do:

"Slater, wake up," my dad said, shaking me. "OK, OK," I said.

"Get up and get dressed," my dad told me.

At school, I was nervous. The morning classes were fine, and so was recess. Then we came to lunch. I was sitting between Eddy and Billy. Billy said some really nasty and hurtful things to Eddy.

Anger welled up inside me. I felt like I was steaming. Then I blurted out, "Pick on somebody your own size!"

The truth was that they were actually the same age, so at first Billy laughed. Then he saw that I wasn't laughing. I had said something funny, but at least I proved my point. Billy stayed quiet for the rest of the day.

I arrived at school the next day, and both teachers had a meeting early in the morning. It was very unusual, especially to have the meeting in the morning. People were coming in and out of the classroom. Then I realized that the teachers were dealing with Eddy and Billy.

I was called down.

I told the teachers everything that happened. Billy was punished and learned his lesson. He also apologized. He actually became friendly with Eddy.

That afternoon, I went home on the bus. When I got off the bus and saw my mom she asked, "How was school today?"

"Great, mom," I replied, and we walked home.

The Courage of Boston's Children, Volume XVII, The Max Warburg Courage Curriculum and the Boston Public Schools, Northeastern University, 2008.

1. Describe the student who was bullied.

_____

_____

_____

2. Describe the behavior of those who were bullying.

_____

_____

_____

3. Describe how Slater helped the student who was bullied.

_____

_____

_____

4. On a separate sheet of paper draw a picture to show how Slater helped Eddy.

5. Prepare to tell the story of how Slater helped Eddy. Include in your storytelling, a description of the person who was treated with disrespect, the behavior of those who were disrespectful, and Slater's actions.

6. Tell Slater's story to your class and possibly other audiences.

GUIVENS

Courage in My Life

I remember lunchtime in my K2 class many years ago in Haiti. I had this friend who would always bring his own lunch to school. We shared and traded what we didn't like on a regular basis.

One day three boys came and took my friend's lunch. When I saw this I thought it was nonsense. I pleaded with him to tell the teacher but he was too scared to move. This kept happening day after day. Soon the boys started getting accustomed to it.

Never in a day would the bullies stop. They could not resist doing it.

It was like a temptation. The worst part was that this became pervasive, happening every day. I went home angry and upset. I told myself I'd have to do something about it. It was a challenge but I couldn't stand to watch it any more.

"Give me your lunch," one of them said. Now my friend is a small guy, so small you could walk right by and not see him. So, he fought while tucking his lunch box under his arm. Being so small and weak did not help, and so the lunch box came flying out.

They started running away when I hollered out. They turned and I began walking toward them. This is when I realized I wasn't the biggest guy in the world either. I felt so small as they got closer to me. I wanted to go back and get myself out of the situation, but I remembered that I had to do it for my friend.

I could see the scorn on their faces. I had so much confidence and courage. When I got to them I said, "You want lunch? Why don't you get your own? If you ever take anyone's personal property in this school again you will regret it."

You should have seen their faces. They were covered with shock and fear from head to toe. He handed me the lunch box and we became friends. I was glad I put a conclusion to that. To me that was the pinnacle point of my school days in Haiti.

The Courage of Boston's Children, Volume XVI, The Max Warburg Courage Curriculum, Inc. and the Boston Public Schools, Houghton Mifflin Company, 2007.

1. Describe the student who was bullied.

_____

_____

_____

2. Describe the behavior of those who were bullying.

_____

_____

_____

3. Describe how Guivens helped his friend who was bullied.

_____

_____

_____

4. On a separate sheet of paper draw a picture to show how Guivens helped his friend.

5. Prepare to tell the story of how Guivens helped his friend. Include in your storytelling, a description of the person who was treated with disrespect, the behavior of those who were disrespectful, and Guivens's actions.

6. Tell Guivens's story to your class and possibly other audiences.

CHRISTINA

Courage in My Life

Courage to me is not just being brave, but is also standing up for what you believe is right. It's like the time back in third grade when I was nine years old. It all started when I went to the after school program at the Ohrenburger School. I was working on my math homework, trying to finish all of it while talking to a friend, when something caught my eye. I looked over at the lunch tables near the doors and saw these kids picking on special needs children. Then as I kept looking, I saw tears coming down the special needs children's faces. I too felt like I was going to drop down to the floor and cry because the other kids were being so mean. Right then and there I knew I had to do something about it. I walked over there calmly and asked, "Can you please stop?" No answer came back. Instead they just laughed at me. That's when courage that I didn't even know I had came out.

"What you are doing is very wrong, you wouldn't like people to treat you like that! Now would you?" Finally the kids stopped. I went over to the special needs children and sat, talked, and played with them for awhile. They began to cheer up after awhile and become more happy.

Since that day, I realized one thing, no matter what other people think, you must make your own decision based on what you believe. That is what courage is all about!

Courage of Boston's Children, Volume XIV, The Max Warburg Courage Curriculum, Inc. and the Boston Public Schools, Houghton Mifflin Company, 2005.

1. What do you think the kids were doing when they "were being so mean"?

_____

_____

_____

2. Describe how Christina helped others.

_____

_____

_____

3. On a separate sheet of paper draw a picture to show how Christina helped other children.

4. Prepare to tell the story of how Christina helped other children. Include in your storytelling, a description of the person who was treated with disrespect, the behavior of those who were disrespectful, and Christina's actions.

5. Tell Christina's story to your class and possibly other audiences.

HOLLY

Courage in My Life

Courage, it's a simple thing actually. Some people might say it's like jumping off of a bridge because of a dare. Some would say it's all about taking a risk. They're wrong. Yes, courage means a risk but not just that. It also takes a good, powerful reason for doing what you did that is courageous. You shouldn't do it for selfish reasons. You should do it for someone else's sake. You shouldn't take courage for granted. I know I didn't.

Third grade was a bad year for me, but one person turned it around. I was new and everyone was always staring at me. It was an unsettling year, but then I met a boy who also needed help like I did. The only thing that was different was that he was slightly mentally challenged and overweight. He was the nicest, friendliest person I ever met. Everyone always made fun of him, and I realized that he had it much worse than I did. I would rather people ignore me than make fun of me and be riding me every second. From there on I helped him and I stood up for him.

One day I thought it was out of my hands. The three boys who always made fun of him the most were following him around all day long. They were calling him names; I didn't want to get in the middle of it. I didn't help him or stand up for him. I felt so terrible after that. At lunch he ran out the door pretending he was going to the bathroom but I knew he wasn't. I went after him to find him sitting on the floor next to the water bubbler crying. At that moment the world stopped, and I focused my mind on him. I never felt my stomach drop like it did that day. I sat down next to him. We didn't talk for a while. We just sat there.

I guess me sitting with him healed him a little; he stopped crying. Then we talked. We talked about everything, about home and school and grades. I never knew it hurt him so much to be made fun of. He never showed any sign that it bothered him. I helped him without even knowing it. I made someone stop crying. It felt good. I told him that he was better than those boys put together. He had to be strong and stand up to them himself. He, who was hiding behind me, realized he couldn't hide forever. He had to feel courage and he had to face them on his own. He did and they stopped hurting him with their nicknames and their rude comments.

I thought maybe if I helped someone, I'd have a good reputation, but something so selfish turned into something great. I did ask myself what I was getting into, but that question turned into an answer. I hated what those boys did to him. I knew that I had to find a way to stop it, and in a way, I did. After the talk we had, the boys never really bothered him as much. I'm happy I helped him. It was courageous because I took a risk. My risk was just to be hated by those boys, and they probably would have made fun of me. I would have been in his position, but my reason was truly to help a boy in need.

The Courage of Boston's Children, Volume XIV, The Max Warburg Courage Curriculum, Inc. and the Boston Public Schools, Houghton Mifflin Company, 2005.

1. Describe the behavior of the one who was bullied.

_____

_____

_____

2. Describe the behavior of those who were bullying.

_____

_____

_____

3. Describe Holly's behavior.

_____

_____

_____

4. On a separate sheet of paper draw a picture to show how Holly helped a boy at school.

5. Prepare to tell the story of how Holly helped her schoolmate. Include in your storytelling, a description of the person who was treated with disrespect, the behavior of those who were disrespectful, and Holly's actions.

6. Tell Holly's story to your class and possibly other audiences.

LATOYA

Courage in My Life

Courage for me is to be able to show people what I stand for and what I can do to protect my friends and family. For me as a student, I show a lot of courage to all my friends and fellow students.

I knew there would be harder work and I'd have to meet new people and make new friends at my new school. People told me there would be a lot of teasing and bullying in middle school but I didn't believe them. Then when I got there, I found out it was true.

At my school, which is near the Fields Corner MBTA station, there is so much teasing and bullying that a lot of my friends are hurt by. This upsets me a lot.

One of my classmates has been teased since the beginning of the school year. The boys from my classroom call her names, they make fun of her clothes, they talk about her weight and they are extremely mean to her.

I've tried to help her by telling the teacher and talking to her about how different we are from each other. Even though my teacher took some time to talk to the boys, I personally stood up for her by confronting the boys. I told them to leave her alone. They wouldn't even listen to me but then the Assistant Principal spoke to them. They listened to her!

Courage to me means to stand up to the bullies and not be afraid of anything that comes my way. By doing that I hope as I grow older, I will become more sensitive of other people's problems.

Then I will be able to do my part to make this a better world.

The Courage of Boston's Children, Volume XIV, The Max Warburg Courage Curriculum, Inc. and the Boston Public Schools, Houghton Mifflin Company, 2005.

1. Describe the one who was bullied.

_____

_____

_____

2. Describe the behavior of those who were bullying.

_____

_____

_____

3. Describe how Latoya helped her friend.

_____

_____

_____

4. On a separate sheet of paper draw a picture to show how Latoya helped her friend.

5. Prepare to tell the story of how Latoya helped her friend. Include in your storytelling, a description of the person who was treated with disrespect, the behavior of those who were disrespectful, and Latoya's actions.

6. Tell Latoya's story to your class and possibly other audiences.

CRYSTAL

Courage in My Life

Courage! When you think of the word, you probably think of being a hero, but in my case, it's for standing up for what you think is right.

My story goes like this. It was the end of my fifth grade year, and my school decided to take the three fifth grade classes on a trip to New York. Everyone was excited.

We went to New York for three days. On the second night of our stay, our hotel was holding a dance. That night everyone seemed like they were ready to dance the night away. However, when I arrived at the dance, everyone was just sitting around doing nothing. Then the fun began, everyone started having a wonderful time.

After a few dances, I got tired so I sat down. While I was resting, I noticed a few friends of mine laughing like crazy. When I looked to see what they were laughing at, I was so surprised. They were laughing at this handicapped person dancing by himself. Since no one was dancing with me, I went over and danced with him. I really got to know this person, and we became real good friends. My friend and I were having a wonderful time. My old friends called me lots of real mean names, but I did not care. Steven and I danced around the clock.

After my buddy left to go back to his hotel room, my pals started being nice to me again. Some of them asked me why I danced with a retard. I yelled at them and told them that, "Just because Steven cannot do some things that you can do, he is just like you no matter what way you put it."

After that night I never saw Steven again. But I will always remember him because he taught me that even though people are different on the outside, we are all the same on the inside. And that's my story!

The Courage of Boston's Children, Volume II, The Max Warburg Courage Curriculum, Inc. and the Boston Public Schools, Houghton Mifflin Company, 1993.

1. Describe the behavior of those who were treating Steven with disrespect.

_____

_____

_____

2. Describe how Crystal helped Steven.

_____

_____

_____

3. On a separate sheet of paper draw a picture to show how Crystal helped Steven.

4. Prepare to tell the story of how Crystal helped Steven. Include in your storytelling, a description of the person who was treated with disrespect, the behavior of those who were disrespectful, and Crystal's actions.

5. Tell Crystal's story to your class and possibly other audiences.

TODD

Luke was a shy, fearful, and nervous nine-year-old. He had a few friends but mostly children bullied him and called him names like mamma's boy *and* fag. *When the Daniel's family moved next door they invited Luke to play soccer. Luke was embarrassed because he didn't know how to play. Mr. Daniels said "No time like the present to learn."*

Mrs. and Mr. Daniels, their two daughters, and their ten-year-old son Todd did not laugh at Luke but helped him learn. Luke got so good at soccer he was invited to join the team that Todd played on and Mr. Daniels coached.

Some kids on the soccer team were from Luke's school and teased him. Todd told his father, who got the group to sit in a circle. Todd sat next to Luke. Mr. Daniels said that bullying was not allowed on his team. He talked about sportsmanship and asked what kind of a team they would have if he allowed them to disrespect each other. Todd said how he'd felt hearing them tease his new friend.

Mr. Daniels asked Luke to talk about his feelings. Luke was tongue-tied and almost cried. No one had asked him that before. He told the team how he felt and asked them why they were mean to him. One boy said it was because Luke's mom always defended him. Luke said it wasn't his fault. One of the boys apologized. Another talked about how he had felt when he was bullied. Then they started practice, and never picked on Luke again.

Jane Middleton-Moz and Mary Lee Zawadski, adaptation of "Luke's Story" from *Bullies from the Playground to the Boardroom, Strategies for Survival.* Copyright 2002 by Jane Middleton-Moz and Mary Lee Zawadski. Adapted and used with the permission of Health Communications, Inc., www.hcibooks.com.

1. Describe Luke.

_____

_____

_____

2. Describe the behavior of those who were bullying Luke.

_____

_____

_____

3. Describe how Todd stood up for Luke.

_____

_____

_____

4. On a separate sheet of paper draw a picture to show how Todd helped Luke.

5. Prepare to tell the story of how Todd helped Luke. Include in your storytelling, a description of the person who was treated with disrespect, the behavior of those who were disrespectful, and Todd's actions.

6. Tell Todd's story to your class and possibly other audiences.

MARISSA

by Carol Wintle

When Marissa was in third grade she had a habit of chewing on her clothes. At recess she sat on a bench and refused to play. Some children made faces at her and called her ugly. When they did this Marissa unsuccessfully tried to chase and hit them.

One day a boy who was mocking Marissa yelled, "You don't have any friends. You don't have any friends." All of a sudden a group of students from Marissa's class stood between Marissa and the boy. They calmly said to the boy, "Stop that."

Even though these children were in the same classroom as Marissa they had not spent time with her at recess before. When the students were back in their class they went with Marissa to tell their teacher what had happened. The teacher, Marissa, and her helpers problem-solved about what to do and decided that for the next week children would take turns sitting with Marissa at recess. Several days later kids stopped being mean to Marissa and she started playing at recess and having fun.

1. Describe Marissa.

_____

_____

_____

2. Describe the behavior of the children who bullied Marissa.

_____

_____

_____

3. Describe how Marissa's classmates stood up for Marissa.

_____

_____

_____

4. On a separate sheet of paper draw a picture to show how Marissa's classmates helped her.

5. Prepare to tell the story of how Marissa's classmates helped her. Include in your storytelling, a description of the person who was treated with disrespect, the behavior of those who were disrespectful, and her classmates' actions.

6. Tell Marissa's story to your class and possibly other audiences.

SPEAK UP FOR OTHERS #1

This activity requires at least two people: one person reads the disrespectful statements and the other pretends to stick up for someone who is bullied.

When you pretend to speak up for someone who is bullied, stand tall, pull your shoulders back, hold your head high, take a deep breath, and speak in a calm voice without yelling.

Disrespectful Statements	Assertive Responses
He's a momma's boy.	Knock it off.
He's a fag.	We don't hurt people here.
She's a stupid retard.	Stop saying that.
Don't be Charlotte's friend.	I like her.
What on earth is that?	Leave her alone.
That is the ugliest girl I have ever seen.	That's so mean.
How did she get to be so ugly?	I feel mad when I hear you say that.
Avery is a girl.	Stop bothering him.
Pirate, where's your hook?	I don't want to hear that.
Too chicken?	That's not funny.
Are you deaf or just dumb?	That's not cool.
What's wrong with him?	He's just a person like you are.
Avery walks funny.	Go away.
She smells like armpits.	That is not okay.
There goes Fatso.	Call him by his real name.
Slow poke.	I don't like how you are treating her.

After completing this assignment, de-brief by asking each other...

• What did it feel like to read the disrespectful statements?

• What did it feel like to read the assertive statements?

SPEAK UP FOR OTHERS #2

Repeat the *Speak Up for Others #1* activity with a family member, friend, neighbor, or teacher. When you are done, de-brief. Ask your partner how it felt for him or her to read the disrespectful and assertive statements. Record the answers.

1. How did it feel to read the disrespectful statements?

_____

_____

_____

_____

_____

2. How did it feel to read the assertive statements?

_____

_____

_____

_____

_____

3. Circle the correct description of your partner.

Family member: mother   father   sister   brother   grandparent   aunt   uncle   other

friend   neighbor   teacher

EIGHT

Stop Bullying at School

Objectives

- To explore assertive ways to stick up for oneself and others.

- To provide students with a wide variety of illustrations of how they can assertively stick up for themselves when treated with disrespect

- To help students develop assertive communication skills.

- To explore ways children can work with adults to stop bullying at school.

- To involve students in illustrating examples of assertive communication through a variety of art forms such as poems, stories, cartoons, and posters.

Chapter Summary, *Avery Quinn: Flying*

The story ends with Avery getting much more support from his peers. The combination of some adults and students supporting Avery, along with him becoming more confident and skilled is what causes those who were bullying Avery to stop.

Suggestions for Success

1. *Acting* techniques are good for all students in your class to know how to use. Encourage children to handle everyday issues of disrespect with creative approaches such as these. Acting techniques would be difficult however for students who are seriously bullied to use, especially if adults and peers at school do not support them.

   Avery was able to assert himself with his father, and he worked very hard to develop new skills. Acting techniques proved effective for him to a great extent because of the support he received from a few of his peers, a teacher at school, and his father.

2. The Handout: *Stop Bullying* summarizes the concepts in this curriculum. Using this with the Handout: *Nelson* will help reinforce the primary message of this guide which is that students and adults need to work together to successfully stop bullying at school.

Activities

Avery Quinn: Flying

   a. Read the chapter aloud to the class.
   b. Use the Chapter Discussion questions to stimulate conversation about the chapter.

Most of the activities in this section are highly recommended.

1. Role-play: Acting #1

Involve either pairs or the whole class in role-plays. Use approach a or b.

    a. Divide students into pairs. Give each pair a copy of *Acting #1.*

- Explain that one student will read the disrespectful statements and the other pretend to be Avery sticking up for himself.
- Before doing the *Acting* role-plays, lead the class in a *Visualization* exercise. In (parenthesis) are instructions for the teacher. In *italics* are what you say to your class.

    Close your eyes. Take three slow, deep breaths.
      (Pause. Take three slow, deep breaths in and out.)
    Imagine you are being treated disrespectfully by someone at school.
      (Pause. Take two slow, deep breaths in and out.)
    See yourself standing tall with your head up and shoulders back.
      (Pause. Take a slow, deep breath in and out.)
    Hear yourself speaking in a calm yet strong voice.
      (Pause. Take a slow, deep breath in and out.)
    Now stick up for yourself using an acting skill.
      (Pause. Take three slow, deep breaths in and out.)
    When you are ready, slowly open your eyes.
      (Pause until all students have opened their eyes.)
    Stand up and shake out your arms.

- After students complete the role-play once, they switch places. The one who played Avery first now reads the disrespectful statements and vice versa.
- Then students de-brief. They call each other by their real names and ask each other how it felt to read the disrespectful and assertive statements.

    b. A simpler approach, and if the group needs more structure, is for the teacher to read the disrespectful statements and one at a time, or the whole group together, give the assertive responses.

- De-brief. Call the children by their real names. Ask them how it felt to say the assertive responses.

2. Homework: Acting #2

    a. Give each student the Handouts: *Acting #1* and *Acting #2.*

    b. Students repeat the *Acting #1* activity with a family member, friend, neighbor, or teacher and complete and turn in the *Acting #2* handout.

3. Stop Bullying at School

a. Distribute the Handout: *Stop Bullying at School* for students to read individually.

b. Divide the class into groups. Give each group the **Handout: Nelson** to read and complete.

c. Each group verbally presents their story to the class of how they helped Nelson.

d. Staying in character, they respond to questions from classmates.

e. De-brief. Ask children to say their real names and how it felt to pretend to be students in Nelson's school.

4. Review

a. Individually or in pairs, students complete and turn in the Handout: *Review.*

5. Art projects

a. Post the *Stickup for Others* chart.

b. Distribute the Handout: *Who Are the Helpers?*

c. Using these lists as references, students individually or in groups, create stories, puppet shows, poems, posters, or cartoons that show someone assertively sticking up for a person who is treated with disrespect. The goal is to illustrate each of the following examples.

—ask adults for help

—ask or tell children who bully to stop

—say nice things about those who are bullied

—listen and talk to children who are bullied

—sit, stand or walk next to children who are bullied

—invite children who are bullied to do something fun with them, join a game or group activity, and

—tell their friends how they feel when their friends act mean.

d. Each child, or group of students, presents their artistic creations.

e. As a class, choose which of the artistic creations to share with other students at your school. Post *Stick Up for Others* pictures and posters. Go the other classrooms to read poems and stories, and to perform skits.

Avery Quinn: *Flying*

I didn't notice a thing around me when I walked down our driveway the next morning. I was busy making up my own jokes. When the bus pulled up I looked to see if Ryon was sitting in the front row. He wasn't. But somebody else was. A girl. Her straight, shiny hair covered her face.

The girl looked up when I got on the bus. She jumped a little as if she was surprised to see me.

"Want company?" she asked. I hesitated before I sat down.

"My name is Winona," she said. "You're Avery, right?"

"Yeah," I whispered.

"I drew this." She held up a picture of a panther in one hand and some black, brown, and orange markers in the other.

"That's good," I mumbled, in a slightly louder voice.

"This is a Bengal tiger," she said, passing me another picture.

She looked into her backpack and pulled out a sketchbook. The letters WWF were on the cover. She flipped through the pages, showing me her drawings of a kangaroo, an alligator, a monkey, and a crane.

"Animals know when earthquakes and volcano eruptions are about to happen," I said, looking over my shoulder. "If people watch animals they can know when to get away."

"Animals are smart," she said.

I nodded.

Winona followed me off the bus. Ryon, wearing a green and gray soccer jacket ran past.

She pointed at him, "I think that kid has a different soccer outfit for every day of the month."

"I bet his parents are rich," I said.

"He probably shoots birds with a BB gun," she said.

"Yeah," I agreed.

"Oh gosh," said Winona, "I forgot. I've got to run. I'm usually the last one off the bus to give myself more time to draw. But, my teacher told my parents that I'm late for class every morning. I promised them I'd be on time from now on. Sorry I can't walk with you. See you later."

As soon as she left, Carlos, Enzo and Marcella moved in, but without the girls who usually hung around with Carlos.

After lunch I told Mr. Sergio about Winona.

"An ally!" he hollered. "This calls for a celebration!"

I wasn't sure about celebrating but was happy to play Ping-Pong and eat Mr. Sergio's homemade brownies. They were soft and gooey, just the way I like them.

Winona was in the front seat again on the afternoon bus. Ryon was right behind her.

"You can't sit there," he said.

Winona kept her head down and fiddled with her markers until she realized I was there. "Hi," she said, patting the seat next to her, inviting me to sit down.

"You can't sit there," protested Ryon, looking only at Winona.

Winona grinned at me and said, "Nice day, huh?"

She's an actress, I thought, and halfway nodded my head.

"Are you deaf and dumb like him?" demanded Ryon.

Winona handed me a piece of paper. "Here's a picture I drew for you in art class. It's animals running away from a tsunami."

"Thanks," I whispered. I was afraid Ryon would reach over the seat and rip up her picture.

"Know about endangered species?" she asked.

"Some," I said looking back at Ryon. He had moved to another seat.

"I'm a member of the World Wildlife Federation," said Winona, "we try to keep animals from becoming extinct. Me and my twin are new at this school." She lowered her voice and bent her head towards mine. "We didn't get why kids laugh at you. We wanted to help, like Pee Wee Reese did for Jackie Robinson, but weren't sure. When we saw you being brave, we knew we had to be too."

"When Ryon was pushing me, did you yell at him to stop?"

"Yeah we did."

"It helped a lot."

"We planned to sit with you today, but Takoda had to go to the dentist, so I went ahead and did it myself."

I noticed that the words on her tee shirt read *Sioux City 5K Run.* "Are you a runner?" I asked.

"Only when it's a fundraiser for endangered animals," she said. Then she talked for the rest of the bus ride about what I guessed was her favorite topic, animals that are extinct and almost extinct.

The next morning I wore my shirt with a picture on it of the hurricane hunter aircraft Hercules WC-130J flying above a green and white earth. Winona was in the front seat. As soon as I sat down she said, "look," and pointed to the seat behind us. I turned. It was the boy I wanted for a friend.

"This is Takoda," she said, my twin.

They did look alike with the same straight, shiny hair.

"Like his hat?" Winona asked.

I nodded yes.

"I gave it to him for his birthday."

The WWF on Takoda's hat matched the one on the cover of Winona's sketchbook.

When the bus stopped, Winona ran ahead so she wouldn't be late for class. Ryon, sporting a silver and gold soccer jacket jogged past us to the soccer field. Takoda walked with me. I nervously looked around for Carlos and his friends and then back at Takoda. He smiled but didn't say anything. I looked around again for Carlos and then back

at Takoda. I was so happy he was walking with me but felt awkward because we weren't talking. I wondered if he *could* speak. Now that I thought about it Winona had done all the talking.

It's up to me, I told myself.

"Do you like jokes?" I asked.

Takoda nodded.

"Okay. What's the best thing to take into the desert?"

He shrugged his shoulders.

"A thirst aid kit."

He laughed.

I felt encouraged, "What lies at the bottom of the sea and shivers?"

"What?" he asked.

So he can speak, I thought and said, "a nervous wreck."

I looked to see if Enzo and Marcella were following us. They weren't. I told Takoda some more jokes. When we reached our classrooms we parted ways.

I sat at my desk and looked out the window at the empty playground. I imagined myself there, surrounded by friends.

After lunch I went to the gym. A *golden oldies* station blared out of Mr. Sergio's radio. He was shooting hoops and singing along to one of the songs.

"I'm going to recess," I said.

"Have fun, Avery," he called as he dribbled away from me down the court.

I went outside. It was windy and cold. My jacket wasn't warm enough. I thought, *maybe this isn't such a good idea.* I was seriously considering going back inside when Ryon descended on me, just as he and Carlos had my first day of second grade. But Carlos wasn't with him this time, only Enzo. Sunlight bounced off of Ryon's silver and gold jacket.

"If it isn't Wobbly Liver Legs," joked Enzo.

You can do it, I told myself. "Thanks," I said.

"No his name is Fake Leg," laughed Ryon.

"Oh well," I said.

Ryon wagged a finger at me. "We've got plans for you."

"Architectural plans?" I asked. I wondered if I had really said that.

Ryon looked frustrated.

"It's not true that lightning never strikes twice," I said. "A Park Ranger in Virginia was struck by lightning seven times in thirty years."

Enzo's mouth was wide open. I felt like a fast moving stream. Ryon and Enzo were boulders I bounced off of and kept on going.

"Where's your frog hand?" asked Enzo pointing at the left pocket of my jeans.

"Wooden you like to know," I said, smiling at my private joke. I didn't care what they said. I wouldn't let them hurt me like they had before.

"You're not worth our time," said Ryon.

I repeated a Robin Williams line I had memorized, "I'm sorry, if you were right, I'd agree with you."

"Noodle knee," said Enzo.

I knew exactly what I was going to say. "Ah yes the knee. The joint between the thigh and the lower part of a human leg, the hind limb of a vertebrate, the forelimb of a hoofed, four-footed animal, or the tarsal joint of a bird."

"Very funny wise guy," said Ryon.

"What a comedian," said Enzo. Someone pulled on my jacket. It was Takoda. "Want to play Foursquare?" he asked.

"I sure do," I said.

Things changed quickly after that. I had someone to play with at recess and I never sat alone on the bus again. For the next couple of weeks, whenever I was near Carlos, I heard fifth grade girls telling him to leave me alone. It wasn't fun for him, Ryon, Enzo, and Marcella to pick on me anymore, so they stopped.

No longer an easy target, I was the pilot of my own plane, flying high above a green and white earth.

Chapter Discussion

Discuss *Avery Quinn: Flying.*

1. How did Winona and Takoda help Avery?

2. Winona said they wanted to support Avery like Pee Wee Reese did for Jackie Robinson. Does anyone know how Pee Wee Reese helped Jackie Robinson?

3. Why did Ryon, Carlos, Enzo and Marcella stop bullying Avery Quinn?

Empowering Children to Help Stop Bullying at School

ACTING #1

This activity requires at least two people: one person reads the disrespectful statements and the other pretends to be Avery speaking up for himself. When you pretend to be Avery stand tall, pull your shoulders back, hold your head high, take a slow, deep breath, and speak calmly without yelling.

Disrespectful Statements	Assertive Responses
You're lame.	Thanks for the compliment.
Are you a boy or girl?	Look at that airplane. It's right on time. Air France I believe.
Avery's a girl's name.	Off it knock. It off knock. Off knock it. It knock off.
Weirdo	If you think I'm strange, you should see my goat.
Limp leg.	Yes, I've got the limpest leg around.
If it isn't little lonely?	Thanks.
Where's your uniform?	Wooden you like to know.
Fake leg.	Oh well.
I've got plans for you.	Architectural plans?
You're not worth my time.	It's not true that lightning never strikes twice. A Park Ranger in Virginia was struck by lighting seven times in thirty years.
Show us your frog hand.	(Whistle or hum.)

After completing this assignment, de-brief. Call each other by your real names and ask your partner...

• What did it feel like to read the disrespectful statements?
• What did it feel like to read the assertive statements?

ACTING #2

Repeat the *Acting #1* activity with a family member, friend, neighbor, or teacher. When you are done, de-brief. Ask your partner how it felt to read the disrespectful and assertive statements. Record their answers.

1. How did it feel to read the disrespectful statements?

_____

_____

_____

_____

_____

2. How did it feel to read the assertive statements?

_____

_____

_____

_____

_____

3. Circle the correct description of your partner.

Family member:　mother　father　sister　brother　grandparent　aunt　uncle　other

friend　　　neighbor　　　teacher

STOP BULLYING AT SCHOOL

Avery's story has a happy ending. The support he received, from some children and adults combined with his personal power, became so strong that the students who bullied him no longer felt powerful putting him down.

Do you think Ryon and Carlos will find another student to bully, with Enzo and Marcella following along? It would be hard for them to succeed if the students at Parker Elementary School acted assertively and were helpers instead of followers or silent watchers.

Avery chose to spend extra time with Mr. Sergio who taught him how to assert himself. The more Avery practiced and stood up for himself, the more confident he became and the easier it was to make friends. He asked his father to help him too. This resulted in Avery becoming more skilled in telling jokes and using acting as a way to stand up for himself.

One of the fifth grade girls spoke up for Avery. After that she and the other fifth grade girls stopped joining in with Carlos and continued to stand up for Avery. Winona and Takoda became Avery's friends. They sat with him, talked and listened to him, walked with him, and invited him into games.

In schools throughout the world children and adults are working together to stop bullying.

Adults at school are ...

- Leading discussions about how to solve bullying problems.
- Using discipline that is firm, caring, consistent, and not harsh.
- Giving all students positive attention, including those who bully.
- Teaching students who silently watch or are followers of bullying how to help students who are bullied instead.
- Providing support for children who are bullied as well as those that help them.
- Working together with parents to learn how to help stop bullying.

Students are...

- Acting assertively.
- Helping children who are bullied.
- Talking to adults about the bullying they see.
- Making sure that every student at school has a friend.

Classrooms are...

- Creating *Respect Agreements* where students agree to:
  —not leave classmates out of groups, games or activities,
  —say kind things about each other, and
  —speak assertively instead of treating each other with disrespect.

- Having regular *Respect Agreement Meetings* to discuss how to successfully keep their classroom *Respect Agreement*.

- Organizing teams of helpers who make sure that:
  —everyone has someone to sit with at lunch,
  —students who are picked on have someone to stick up for them, and
  —students who have trouble fitting in have someone to say nice things about him or her to other children.

- Reading picture books on bullying with children in younger grades to teach them what bullying is and how it can be blocked.

- Performing skits and puppet shows for students in younger grades on how to help a student who is being bullied.

- Creating poems, posters, cartoons and videos about how to stop bullying to share with others in the school.

Schools are...

- Improving supervision in areas of the school where students report bullying is happening.

- Having "Mix Em Up" days once a month where everybody in the school cafeteria sits next to someone at lunch who they don't usually sit with.

- Giving certificates to students who take an oath to promise to:
  —not bully,
  —not exclude anyone from games, groups and clubs, and
  —assertively help others who are bullied.

- Participating in *Bullying Awareness Week* (usually in October or November).

- Reading the pledge, "I will not use my hands or my words for hurting myself or others" every morning, along with the Pledge of Allegiance.

Bullying does not need to lead to tragedies. Leaders of bullying can be helped to change their ways. Followers can stop following. Silent watchers can start speaking up. Children who are treated with disrespect can act assertively. When children and adults creatively work together, bullying can be stopped.

NELSON

Courage in My Life

Hi, my name is Nelson and I'm 12 years old. I was born with a lot of problems. When I'm by myself, I'm lonely and sad. My feelings are easily hurt because I'm so shy.

If the kids talk about me or make fun of me, I start to cry. I mind my own business. I never bother them or make fun of them. Why do they insist on bothering me? I have always been shy.

I was born without kidneys. My mother gave me one of hers so I could survive. If I'm alone I'm sad because I don't have friends to talk or play with, except for my little brother.

Another problem is I can't see far away...

A lot of 6th grade kids bother me. It makes me unhappy when my classmates say mean stuff. It makes me want to leave 6th grade and never come back.

I told my mother about it. At Open House, my mother came to school and talked to my teacher, Mrs. Guarino. It stopped for a while but then continued.

My mother told me to ignore them. It is not easy to ignore them....

I have courage every day when I come to school and face my classmates when they insult me.

The Courage of Boston's Children, Volume XII, The Max Warburg Courage Curriculum, Inc. and the Boston Public Schools, Houghton Mifflin Company, 2003.

Imagine that you are sixth grade students in the same school where Nelson goes. Write a story about how students and adults at school successfully stop the bullying that Nelson is experiencing.

_____

_____

_____

_____

_____

_____

_____

_____

_____

_____

_____

_____

_____

_____

_____

REVIEW

List five different ways you could assertively stick up for yourself if a student at your school treated you with disrespect.

_____

_____

_____

_____

_____

_____

List five ways you could assertively stick up for a student at your school who was bullied.

_____

_____

_____

_____

_____

Stick Up for Yourself

What to do	What to say
Stand tall with your head held high.	Say nothing. Assertively walk away.
Shrug your shoulders.	Say nothing. Assertively walk away.
Ask adults for help.	
Be an actor.	
Pretend you can't hear.	Say nothing. Find something interesting to look at.
Pretend you are not upset.	*If you want to say that, go ahead.* *Keep talking.* *It doesn't bother me.* *That was fun, but I gotta go.* *I didn't know that.* *You might be right.* *Cool.* *If it gives you pleasure to put me down, you can do it all day long.*
Agree with them.	*You're right.* *That's true.* *I know.* *I see what you mean.* *That's great.*
Say thanks.	*Thanks for noticing.* *How kind of you.* *Thanks for telling me.*
Change the subject or say something unexpected.	*Look at that airplane.* *Water, water everywhere and not a drop to drink.* *Which do you like better dogs or horses?* *What do you think of the President?* *What time is lunch?* *Do you think it's going to snow?* *Are you going on the field trip?*
Say something funny.	*If you think I'm weird, you should see my goat.*
Use "Stonewalling" **(Be like a broken record)**	*So. So. So. So.* *What? What? What?* *Nope. Nope. Nope.* *Stop. Stop. Stop. Stop.* *That's your opinion. That's your opinion.*

What to do	What to say	What to say
Speak up.	*Knock it off.*	*I don't want to.*
	Stop annoying me.	*You can't have my pencil. I need it.*
	Stop it.	*Give it back.*
	Stop bothering me.	*Don't be so bossy.*
	Please stop.	*I want you to stop doing that.*
	Call me by my real name.	*I don't agree.*
	Cut it out.	*I have a different opinion.*
	I don't like that.	*Be fair.*
	Leave me alone.	*How would you like it if I said that to you?*
	Go away.	
	No.	*Is that so?*
	Nope.	*I wish I could, but I can't.*
	No I don't.	*That's nice, but I have to say no.*
	No way.	*I'm not changing my mind.*
	No, but thanks for asking.	*I'm going to pass.*
	Let go.	*Got to go.*
	Quit it.	*See you later.*
	No way, Jose.	*Later.*
	Get your hands off me.	*If I valued your opinion, I would be upset.*
	I don't want to fight.	
	Does it make you feel good to make me feel bad?	*Maybe.*
		Maybe not.
	Friends don't do this to friends.	*Could be.*
	Give that back to me now.	*I could care less what you think.*
	I don't like to be pushed around.	*That wasn't very nice.*
	Stop spreading rumors about me.	*Uh-huh, right, okay, yeah.*
	I don't like what you're doing.	*I'm not a soup can. Don't label me.*
	It's not your business.	*Don't laugh at me.*
	I don't think so.	*Whatever.*
	It's not true.	*Do you believe it?*
	How do you know?	*I don't like it when you say things about me that aren't true.*
	Let's talk about it.	
	I need you to move.	*Are you trying to make yourself look good?*
	I'm the same as you.	
	I dare you to be nice.	*I can't believe you just said that.*
	Is that so?	*Are you having a bad day?*
	Are you trying to hurt my feelings or be my friend?	*Right back at ya.*
		Oh well.
	Ouch! That hurts.	*Wow.*

Empowering Children to Help Stop Bullying at School

What to do		What to say
Ask "W" questions.	Why?	*Why are you picking on me?*
		Why are you being mean to me?
		Why would you say that?
		Why are you doing this?
		Why are you touching me?
		Why should I?
		Why do you think that's true?
		Why are you acting that way?
		Why don't you worry about yourself?
		Why do you care what I wear?
		Why don't you do it yourself?
	Who?	*Who told you that?*
		Who told you I said that?
		Who are you?
	What?	*What are you doing?*
		What did you say?
		What is your name again?
		What's wrong with you?
		What makes you think I'm that way?
		What did I ever do to you?
		What are you talking about?
		What's your problem?
		What else have you noticed?
		What's it going to be today?
		What do you mean?
		What's with you?
		What do you want?
	Was?	*Was that really necessary?*

Call children who bully by their real names.

If the child who bullies you is your friend,
tell him or her how you feel.

Don't respond to a mean phone or text message.
Log off. Turn the phone off.

Make new friends.

Sit tall with your head held high.

Visualize yourself as confident and successful.

Don't let kids who bully keep you from
doing your best.

Stick Up for Others

What you can do	What you can say
Be friendly to children who are bullied. 　Listen to them. 　Invite them to do something fun with you.	
Ask adults for help.	
Don't repeat a rumor.	
Use stonewalling, or be like a broken record.	*Stop. Stop. Stop. Stop.* *Quit it. Quit it. Quit it.* *Leave him alone. Leave her alone.*

Speak up.

Knock it off.	*We don't say that here.*
Call him by his real name.	*If he throws like a girl then he must be good.*
Cut it out.	
I don't like how you are treating her.	*Please stop talking like that.*
Leave him alone.	*I believe you should treat people how you want to be treated.*
Go away.	
No.	*I don't want to play unless she is going to play too.*
Stop it.	*Pick on someone your own size.*
Stop bothering her.	*Can you please stop?*
What you said about him is not true.	*What you are doing is very wrong.*
She's just a girl like you are.	*You wouldn't like people to treat you like that, now would you?*
We don't hurt other people here.	
That's so mean.	*You don't know her to judge her.*
I like him.	*You wouldn't want people picking on you especially if you were new like him.*
You wouldn't want people making fun of you.	
That is not okay.	*If you treat people like that it just means you are jealous or insecure.*
That's not funny.	
That's not cool.	*You've gone too far.*
I don't want to hear that.	*You're hurting him.*
That's so ten minutes ago.	*This is not fair.*
That is so last year.	*Just because he cannot do some things that you can, he is just like you, no matter what way you put it.*
Don't make fun of people like that.	
You really hurt her feelings.	
You better apologize.	*My parents say I can't.*
I feel mad when I hear you say that.	

Empowering Children to Help Stop Bullying at School

What to do		**What to say**
Ask "W" questions.	Why?	*Why Why are you picking on him?*
		Why are you being mean to her?
		Why would you say that about him?
		Why are you doing that to her?
		Why are you touching him?
		Why are you bothering her?
		Why do you make fun of him?
		Why don't you get your own lunch?
	Who?	*Who told you that about her?*
		Who says my friend can't play?
	What?	*What's wrong with you?*
		What are you doing?
		What if that were your sister or mother?
		What has she ever done to you?

NINE

Jackie Robinson

Objective

- To provide information on an historical example of bullying and the role that helpers, assertiveness and courage played in overcoming bullying.

Activities

1. Jackie Robinson
   a. Read the story of *Jackie Robinson* aloud to the class.
   b. Use the Chapter Discussion questions to stimulate conversation about Jackie Robinson.

2. Journals
   Students respond to the following assignment in their journals.
   a. It takes courage to stick up for yourself or someone else. Write about a time in your life that you acted with courage or wished you had.

Jackie Robinson

In 1947, Jackie Robinson became the first black man to play baseball in the all white Major Leagues. His ten-year career in the Major Leagues was so successful that in 1962 he was inducted into baseball's Hall of Fame.

Jackie was a target of bullying. He was intentionally and repeatedly treated with disrespect over and over again by players on his own and opposing teams, spectators, and others.

His teammates refused to sit next to him at meals and circulated a petition to get him thrown off their team. Opposing players called Jackie names, threw balls at his head, and tried to spike him with their shoes. Baseball spectators yelled and taunted him with hateful words. Hotel owners would not rent rooms to him. Restaurant owners would not serve him food. Individuals and groups such as the Ku Klux Klan threatened to kill him.

There were those who saw how Jackie was treated and did nothing to help. Some silent witnesses didn't care or were too busy; others felt powerless or afraid to get involved.

Fortunately there were helpers such as Jackie's wife, cheering spectators, people who wrote letters of encouragement, and journalists who spoke up for him. Branch Rickey, general manager of the Brooklyn Dodgers, was a helper. Branch believed in equal opportunities for blacks and whites. He searched for a star athlete in the all black baseball league, found Jackie and hired him. Despite over-whelming protests against his decision, Branch did not give up on Jackie, even when the Brooklyn Dodgers team petitioned him to do just that.

Another helper was Pee Wee Reese. He was the only Dodger who refused to sign the petition to get Jackie Robinson fired. He spoke up for Jackie, saying what a good player he was and how he could help the team win. Once during a game in Pee Wee Reese's hometown, Pee Wee stood with his arm around Jackie's shoulders to show the bullies that he stood by this man. Pee Wee's action was so powerful that it silenced the hostile crowd.

Jackie was not passive or annoying. He asserted his right to be treated as an equal. He was very angry, but his self-control was unbelievably strong. In the words of Branch Rickey, Jackie had the "guts enough not to fight back."

Jackie was not *as calm as the eye of a hurricane*, but he acted as if he was. He stood tall with his shoulders back, did not give up, and powerfully fought against prejudice and hate by playing the best baseball he possibly could.

Discussion: Jackie Robinson

Discuss the story of Jackie Robinson.

1. How was Jackie Robinson treated with disrespect?

2. What do you think he did to keep himself from getting into fights with people who bullied him?

3. What were the characteristics of the helpers Branch Rickey and Pee Wee Reese?

Empowering Children to Help Stop Bullying at School

TEN

Books, Essays & Stories About Bullying

Activities

1. Books, Essays & Stories About Bullying

    a. Have books from the school and public library available for students to choose from, or create a list from the *Books on Bullying* for children to find on their own. The stories and the "Courage in My Life" essays can also be used as well as any that appeared previously in this book.

    b. Students draw numbers to see which child or group chooses a book, story or essay first and so on.

    c. Those interested in reporting on books that are not included in *Empowering Children to Help Stop Bullying* need to receive approval before completing their reports.

    d. Provide each student, or group with the Handouts: *Bullying Book Report, Bullying Book Report Sample,* or *Bullying Story or Essay Report* and *Bullying Story or Essay Report Sample,* depending on what they chose to read.

    e. Students, or groups, hand in their completed *Bullying Book, Story, or Essay Reports.*

    f. Each student, or group, gives an oral presentation of their book, story or essay report. After each presentation, individual students or groups respond to questions from their classmates.

2. Journals

    Students respond in their journals to the following assignment.

    a. Describe a story that a classmate reported on and tell what you
        • liked about the story, or
        • didn't like about the story.

> The literature listed in *Books on Bullying* covers a variety of topics and has examples of bullying portrayed within. The list primarily includes picture books and middle grade fiction. A few young adult novels are included for more advanced readers. The solutions portrayed in these books are ones reflective of the non-violent strategies presented in this curriculum.
>
> Books that present physical aggression as a solution to bullying such as *Indigo's Star,* and *What a Wimp* are not included. Nor are ones such as *How I Survived Fifth Grade, Gopher Takes Heart,* and *The 18th Emergency* that encourage a child who is bullied to dare a leader of bullying to beat them up.

BULLYING BOOK REPORT (Sample)

Read one of the books on bullying. List the title and author.

Title: *Molly's Pilgrim*

Author: *Barbara Cohen*

1. Summarize the story. Describe the bullying that was presented in the story. Identify leaders and followers of bullying, who is bullied, who watches, and who helps.

   Molly is a new student from Russia and the only Jewish child in her third grade class. Her English isn't as good as her classmates.

   Elizabeth bullies Molly. She laughs at how Molly talks and tells her she is dumb. Elizabeth made up a teasing song: "You talk funny Molly. You look funny Molly, Jol-ly Mol-ly. Your eyes are awf'ly small. Jol-ly Mol-ly. Your nose is awf'ly tall."

   Hilda, Kitty and others in the class join in with Elizabeth, laugh at Molly and sing the teasing song.

2. Did anyone try to stop the bullying? If so, how? If not, why not?

   The teacher, Miss Stickley stuck up for Molly and said nice things about her.

3. If you were the author of this book, would you have ended the story differently? Describe how you would have ended the story or explain what you liked about how the story ended.

   Molly is happy at the end and one of her classmates is nice to her. I like the way Mrs. Stickley stuck up for Molly.

Empowering Children to Help Stop Bullying at School

BULLYING BOOK REPORT

Read one of the books on bullying. List the title and author.

Title _____

Author _____

1. Summarize the story. Describe the bullying that was presented in the story. Identify leaders and followers of bullying, who is bullied, who watches, and who helps.

_____
_____
_____
_____
_____
_____
_____
_____
_____

2. Did anyone try to stop the bullying? If so, how? If not, why not?

_____
_____
_____
_____
_____

3. If you were the author of the book would you have ended the story differently? Describe how you would have ended the story or explain what you liked about how the story ended.

_____
_____
_____
_____
_____

BULLYING STORY OR ESSAY REPORT (Sample)

Read one of the Stories or Essays on Bullying. List the title and author.

Title: *Courage in My Life*

Author: *Thomas*

1. Describe the behavior of those who bullied.

   Thomas along with his "cool" friends bullied kids ever since he was in first grade. He called children names, made fun of their weight, and made some so embarrassed that they cried.

2. Describe how the child who was bullied and helpers tried to stop the bullying.

   Thomas became a helper and told his friends that they had gone too far and what they had done had hurt Will really bad. Thomas apologized to Will and became friends with him. He hung out with Will when people tried to tease him.

3. Explain what you liked or didn't like about how the child who was bullied and helpers tried to stop the bullying.

   I liked it that Thomas apologized to Will and became his friend. It's nice to know that kids who bully can become helpers. I agree with Thomas when he said that "if more people stood up for the Wills in this world, this world would be a better place."

BULLYING STORY OR ESSAY REPORT

Read one of the stories or essays on bullying. List the title and author.

Title _____

Author _____

1. Describe the behavior of those who bullied.

_____
_____
_____
_____
_____
_____

2. Describe how the child who was bullied and helpers tried to stop the bullying.

_____
_____
_____
_____
_____
_____

3. Explain what you liked or didn't like about how the child who was bullied and helpers tried to stop the bullying.

_____
_____
_____
_____
_____
_____

Books on Bullying

Picture Books

Alexander, Martha. *Move Over Twerp*. Dial Press, 1981.

Jeffrey is younger and smaller than his schoolmates who bully him on the school bus, but that doesn't stop him from assertively sticking up for himself.

Berenstain, Stan and Jan. *Berenstain Bears and the In-Crowd*, Random House, 1989.

Sister Bear experiences bullying. She explores different ways to respond and finds her own way to make it stop.

Boyd, Lizi. *Bailey, The Big Bully*. Penguin, 1989, 1991.

Bailey is big and mean. All the kids are afraid of him except Max who has no problem sticking up for himself.

Caseley, Judith. *Bully*, Greenwillow Books, 2001.

A child who is bullied and the boy who bullies him become friends.

Cosby, Bill. *The Meanest Thing to Say*, Scholastic Inc., 1997.

This story demonstrates how to use stonewalling by responding to mean words with the repetitive answer, "So."

de paola, Tomie. *Oliver Button is a Sissy*. Harcourt Brace Jovanovich, 1979.

Older boys pick on Oliver because he takes dance lessons. Girls stick up for Oliver and Oliver, with his parents' help, finds a way to stick up for himself.

Giovanni, Nikki. *Rosa*. Henry Holt and Company, 2005.

Rosa Parks stands up for herself and other African Americans who repeatedly are treated with disrespect.

Goldenbock, Peter. *Teammates*. Harcourt Brace Jovanovich, 1990.

Jackie Robinson is bullied when he joins the Brooklyn Dodgers and becomes the first black player in Major League baseball. His white teammate Pee Wee Reese stands up for him.

Hayes, Joe. *No Way, Jose!*. Trails West Publishing, 1986.

Rooster is bossy. When he tells other animals what to do, they assertively stick up for themselves by saying, "No Way, Jose!"

Henkes, Kevin. *Chrysanthemum*. Mulberry Books, 1991.

Chrysanthemum is bullied by her Kindergarten classmates. A teacher sticks up for her and the bullying stops.

Kasza, Keiko. *The Rat and the Tiger*, The Putman & Grosset Group, 1993.

Rat is bullied by his friend Tiger until he finally speaks up for himself.

Lonczak, Heather. *Mookey the Monkey Gets Over Being Teased*. Magination Press, 2007.

A monkey is called baldy by his classmates because he has no hair. His friends help him feel good about who he is.

Lovell, Patty. *Stand Tall, Molly Lou Melon*, G.P. Putman & Sons, 2001.

Molly Lou Melon was the shortest girl in the first grade, had buckteeth, a voice that sounded like a bullfrog, and was clumsy. When she moved to a new school, Ronald Durkin bullied her. But Molly put a stop to the bullying because she was confident and assertive and used her talents and humor, just as her grandmother had taught her to do.

Ludwig, Trudy. *Just Kidding*. Tricycle Press, 2006.

A child who says he is just kidding treats Vince with disrespect. Vince learns how to stick up for himself and someone else too.

Ludwig, Trudy. *My Secret Bully.* Tricycle Press, 2004.

Monica has a friend who bullies her. Her mother helps her decide what to do.

Ludwig, Trudy. *Sorry!* Tricycle Press, 2006.

A boy who is bullied learns how to stick up for himself and someone else too.

Ludwig, Trudy. *Trouble Talk,* Tricycle Press, 2008.

Maya's friend Bailey says mean things, acts rude, and spreads hurtful rumors about Maya and her other friends. Maya tells her to stop but Bailey doesn't listen. The school Counselor helps Maya, her friends and Bailey too.

Madonna. *Mr. Peabody's Apples,* Callaway Editions, 2003.

A boy starts a rumor that ruins the reputation of his baseball coach. The coach effectively teaches the boy how powerfully hurtful rumors are. The boy does his best to correct his mistake.

McCain, Becky Ray. *Nobody knew what to do: a story about bullying.* Albert Whitman & Company, 2001.

A boy witnesses a classmate being bullied and decides what to do.

McLelland, Michael J. *Beating the Bully,* Cedar Fort Inc., 2007.

A boy who is bullied and the one who bullies him become friends.

Moss, Marissa. *Amelia's Bully Survival Guide,* Simon & Schuster Books for Young Readers, 1998.

Written in a similar style as *Diary of a Wimp,* fifth grader Amelia keeps a journal of how, after losing her best friend, a classmate named Hilary starts picking on her every day. Amelia struggles with this experience until she finds an assertive way to make the bullying stop.

Moss, Peggy and Tardif, Dee Dee. *Our Friendship Rules,* Tilbury House Publishers, 2004.

This is a story of relational bullying. It illustrates the problem of losing a "best friend" to someone more "cool" and being shunned, with a solution involving assertive communication, problem-solving, and reconciliation.

Moss, Peggy. *Say something.* Tilbury House Publishers, 2004.

A girl silently witnesses bullying at her school, then she gets bullied too and finds a way to cope.

Mochizuki, Ken. *Baseball Saved Us.* Lee & Low, 1993.

Shorty is a Japanese American during World War II. His classmates call him "Jap." He is the last to be picked for teams. No one is friendly towards him. He has to eat lunch by himself. Shorty's family and community help him become good at playing baseball and with those skills he finds a way to belong.

O'Neil, Alexis. *The Recess Queen.* Scholastic Press, 2002.

Mean Jean bullies the kids at school, but Katie Sue, the new girl, knows just what to do.

Palacco, Patricia. *Mr. Lincoln's Way,* Philomel Books, 2001.

A school Principal helps a boy who bullies to change.

Rosenberg, Liz. *Monster Mama.* Putnam, 1993.

Patrick Edward is bullied. His mother helps him out.

Whitcomb, Mary. *Odd Velvet.* Chronicle Books, 1998.

Velvet is odd. At first no one wants to play with her, but once they get to know her, they change their minds.

Zolotow, Charlotte. *The Hating Book,* Harper Trophy, 1969.

Written for young children, this book illustrates some aspects of relational bullying and the power of asking "Why?"

Chapter Books and Novels

Bao Lord, Bette. *In the Year of the Boar and Jackie Robinson.* Harper Trophy/Harper Collins, 1984.

Shirley Temple Wong is bullied because she is from China, can't speak much English and doesn't know the customs.

Bosch, Carl. *Bully on the Bus.* Parenting Press, 1988.

Fifth grader, Nick Jones throws spit wads on the bus, calls people names, and threatens to punch kids in the face. The reader chooses what to do.

Bruchac, Joseph. *Eagle Song*. Dial Books for Young Readers, 1997.
    Tyrone and other boys at school bully Danny Bigtree because he is a Native American. His father helps him find a strong, successful way to stick up for himself.

Clements, Andrew. *Jake Drake, Bully Buster*. Simon & Schuster Books for Young Readers, 2001.
    Second grader Jake Drake acts passively and is bullied by many students including Superbully, Link Baxter. When Jake asserts himself things change for the better.

Cohen, Barbara. *Molly's Pilgrim*. Bantum Books, 1983.
    Molly and her family move to America from Russia. The children in her third grade class make fun of her accent and clothes. Molly's teacher sticks up for her and the bullying stops.

Cole, Joanna. *Don't Call Me Names*. Random House, 1990.
    Nell is afraid of Mike and Joe because they always make fun of her. Then one day she stands up to them on behalf of her friend Nicky.

DiCamillo, Kate. *Because of Winn-Dixie*, Candlewick Press, 2000.
    This story about a girl and her dog includes some bullying scenes. Opal learns to stop responding to aggression with aggression and to assertively act friendly instead.

dePino, Catherine. *Blue Cheese Breath and Stinky Feet—How to deal with bullies*. Magination Press, 2004.
    Steve is bullied by Gus and isn't sure what to do. He and his parents come up with a plan for Gus to stick up for himself.

Estes, Eleanor. *The Hundred Dresses*. Harcourt Brace Jovanovich, 1944.
    Maddie silently watches her friends bully a classmate. She wishes she had the courage to be a helper instead.

Greenfield, Eloise. *Rosa Parks*. Harper Trophy, 1973.
    Rosa Parks stands up for herself and other African Americans who repeatedly are treated with disrespect.

Hines, Anna Grossnickle. *Tell Me Your Best Thing*. Penguin Group, 1990.
    Third grader Charlotte invites Sophie to join her club, then bullies her. In this example of relational bullying, which is most common with girls, Sophie learns how to stick up for herself.

Kinsey-Warnock, Natalie. *The Night the Bells Rang*, Cobblehill Books, 1991.
    This story takes place in 1918 in Northern Vermont. Mason is bullied at school by Aden and unable to stick up for himself. Mason takes out his frustration on his younger brother. A turn of events teaches Mason that there is another side of Aden as well as himself.

Levy, Elizabeth. *Third Grade Bullies*, Hyperion Books for Children, 1998.
    Third graders learn how to assertively stick up for themselves and others.

Lowry, Lois. *Number the stars*. Dell, 1990.
    In 1943, during the German occupation of Denmark, ten-year-old Annemarie learns how to be brave and courageous when she helps shelter her Jewish friend from the Nazis.

Maddox, Jake. *On the Line*. Stone Arch Books, 2007.
    This story explores the relationship of a boy who bullies and the boy he bullies. They eventually become teammates.

Millman, Dan. *Secret of the Peaceful Warrior*. Starseed Press, 1991.
    A wise man named Socrates shows Danny how to be a peaceful warrior and respond to bullying with courage, assertiveness and respect.

Paterson, Katherine. *Bridge to Terabithia*. Harper Trophy, 1987.
    Jess and Leslie are bullied at school. They stick up for each other by becoming friends.

Paterson, Katherine. *The great Gilly Hopkins*. Cornerstone Books, 1987.
    When Gilly comes to live at her new foster home, she bullies another child. Eventually she stops and becomes a helper instead.

Patneaude, David. *Colder Than Ice*. Albert Whitman, 2003.

> Josh, a sixth grader is overweight and a new student at school. He is tempted to join in with bullying so he will look cool. His true friends, children who are also bullied, help Josh make a better choice.

Poole, Josephine. *Anne Frank*. Alfred A. Knopf, 2005.

> This book for children ages eight and older tells the life story of Anne Frank. Included in this historic portrayal are the Nazis, those who joined with the Nazis, those who silently watched, the victims, and those who helped the victims.

Robinson, Nancy. *Wendy and the Bullies*. Scholastic, 1991.

> Wendy explores ways to assertively deal with bullies.

Rowan Masters, Susan. *The Secret Life of Hubie Hartzel*. Lippincott, 1990.

> 5th grader Hubie is bullied. His father shows him what he can do to keep himself out of a fight.

Shreve, Susan. *Joshua T. Bates Takes Charge*. Knopf, 1993.

> Eleven-year-old Joshua silently watches a classmate being bullied and decides to help.

Spinelli, Jerry. *Loser*. Joanna Cotler Books, 2002.

> Zinkoff is bullied and sticks up for himself.

Stolz, Mary. *The Bully of Barkham Street*. Harper Collins, 1985.

> A child who bullies talks about himself.

Taylor, Mildred D. *The Well*. Puffin Books, 1998.

> White boys bully black boys and get punished for it.

White Pellegrino, *Marjorie. Too Nice*. Magination Press, 2002.

> A girl who is too nice gets bullied, then learns how to stand up for herself.

Wilson Wesley, Valeria. *How to Face Up to the Class Bully*, Jump at the Sun, Hyperion Books for Children, 2007.

> Irene, a new girl at school, bullies Willamena. At first Willamena acts passive, then aggressive. Her assertive actions help other children speak up. The problem is solved and Irene learns to treat her classmates with respect.

Winthrop, Elizabeth. *Luke's Bully*. Penguin Group, 1990.

> Skinny, shy third-grader Luke is bullied by Arthur. Luke finds a way to become friends instead.

Yashima, Taro, *Crow Boy*. Puffin Books, 1955, 1983.

> Chibi has no friends and is called names. A teacher helps him and the bullying stops.

Zeier, Joan. *Stick Boy*. Athenaeum, 1993.

> Skinny sixth grader Eric is bullied.

Zindel, Paul. *Attack of the Killer Fishsticks*. Skylark Books, 1993.

> Fifth graders, Dave, Jennifer, Johnny, and Liz stick up for Max, a new student at their school who wears a tie and is bullied. They also invite Max to join their Wacky Facts Lunch Bunch club.

Young Adult

Adler, C.S. *The Once in a while hero*. Coward, McCann & Geoghegan, 1982.

> A gentle and sensitive seventh grader struggles to stand up to a bully in his class and discovers how, by sticking up for a new boy at his school.

Bryont, Annie. *Lake Rescue*. Beacon Street Girls, B'tween Productions, Inc. 2005.

> Chelsea, an overweight girl, is bullied. A group of middle school students called the Beacon Street Girls, and a kind adult, help her out.

Howe, James. *the misfits*. Aladdin Paperbacks, 2001.

> Four students who do not fit in at their middle school create a third party for the Student Council elections to represent all young people who have ever been called names.

Essays: Courage in My Life

Ciboney was called names and given dirty looks. She spoke up for herself and talked to a teacher.

Andre was made fun of because he couldn't read well. His brother and sister gave him advice. He worked hard to become a good reader.

Jalil was called *midget*. She ignored those who bullied her and didn't let them keep her from doing her best.

Rhoderick was called names. He spoke to his mother and teachers who helped him.

Samantha was called *fatty*. She spoke with her parents who gave her support.

Sei's cousin Flamo was new to America and didn't speak much English. Classmates laughed at his name. Sei listened to Flamo and advised him on how to get by.

Tsega heard that a student was planning to throw a milk box at a girl who got a good score on a test. Tsega jumped in the way so the milk spilled on him instead.

Shelly was spit on and had rocks thrown at her. She told a teacher who helped her.

Empowering Children to Help Stop Bullying at School

CIBONEY

Courage in My Life

Courage means being brave and knowing how to stand up for one's self. There are many brave people from our past, present and hopefully in the future. Martin Luther King, Jr. is a perfect example of someone who showed courage, because he stood up for himself and others, without using violence. Courage cannot take place while sitting down and hoping to be brave. Instead, courage comes through when we get up and stand up for what we know is right.

When I was in the fifth grade, I was a good student. I always behaved myself, no matter what anyone else was doing. My fifth grade teacher had a rewards system for my class. At the end of each day, she would put a check next to the names of every student who did well and behaved. I received one every day.

One day, when we were outside for recess, some of the girls from my class called me over to a corner and asked me why I always do the right thing, and always complete my work. I told them I do this because I want to be able to go to sixth grade. Then they asked me, "Why don't you stop being so good for a while, and just be bad like us?" I asked them why they like to behave that way, and they responded with, "Because it's fun, and that's how we roll!" I explained that I didn't want to be in their little group because I like making the right choices, and then walked away.

From that day on, every time I saw these girls, they called me names and gave me dirty looks. I made sure to ignore them and continue my quest to accomplish my goals, follow my dreams, and stay on the right path.

I showed courage by standing up for and doing what is right. I also showed courage by ignoring those girls and talking to a teacher about what happened, rather than turning to violence.

The Courage of Boston's Children, Volume XVII, The Max Warburg Courage Curriculum, Inc. and the Boston Public Schools, Northeastern University, 2008.

ANDRE

Courage in My Life

My name is Andre Conway, and I am a sixth grader at the Sarah Greenwood School. To me, courage is when you stand up for yourself. I am going to tell you about a time I showed courage.

It was my first day at the Sarah Greenwood School. People picked on me because I could not read. Hearing this, my brother and sister gave me some advice: that I should study hard, forget what the other kids say, and ignore them.

The next day I went back to school. As usual, kids picked on me. This time, I used my brother's and sister's advice and ignored them. Then I went back to my desk and studied some cards. Over the next weeks I studied at home and at school. At school, I would sit on the rug and practice some flash cards. I would sound out the words. At home I would read two books before I went to sleep every night.

I feel that if it weren't for my second grade teacher, Ms. Alongi, I would never be where I am four years later. Now I am in the sixth grade, and every time I see a word, I know how to say it and what it means. Now when I am in class no one picks on me, because I am a good reader. Instead of kids picking on me, they're my friends.

It did not feel good when kids picked on me. Instead of being mean back to them, I worked hard and showed courage.

The Courage of Boston's Children, Volume XVII, The Max Warburg Courage Curriculum, Inc. and the Boston Public Schools, Northeastern University, 2008.

JALIL

Courage in My Life

Courage to me means doing something brave that no one else would or wanted to do. This I know because I did something incredibly courageous at the age of six.

When I was just six years old going on seven and in the first grade, I loved to dance. I would practice dancing at home all the time with the music blasting so loudly that the whole street could hear it. Many people at my school knew that I had talent, but instead of admitting it, they would just tease me about my height. But I didn't let that bring me down from doing what I loved to do.

One day at dismissal, just the usual boring day, a blizzard was beginning outside, so the students who took the bus had to go into the auditorium. Due to the bad weather we had to stay in a bit longer, so my science teacher suggested that, instead of boring ourselves while waiting for the buses to arrive, we should get some kids to dance. I volunteered almost immediately and began walking towards the stage.

I could hear the fourth- and fifth-graders starting to make fun of me again by saying I'm short and look like a midget. I wanted to turn around and walk back to my seat, but there was no way I was going to let some annoying fourth and fifth graders bring me down with their rude comments and insults. Next thing I knew, I found myself taking off my bag and coat. As the music went on, I started to dance fast. When I was finished dancing, everyone began clapping, including some of the big kids. My science teacher told me that I did a good job dancing and ignoring the older kids' comments. Finally, the buses arrived and I walked on the bus with a smile on my face and said to myself, "It feels good to shut up a bunch of big kids."

It wasn't the fact that I danced in front of a huge crowd that made me courageous, but it was the fact that I ignored people who tried to bring me down and managed to dance even with their insults. That made me courageous.

The Courage of Boston's Children, Volume XVII, The Max Warburg Courage Curriculum, Inc. and the Boston Public Schools, Northeastern University, 2008.

RHODERICK

Courage in My Life

I knew I was different from the way that I walked, talked, and acted. But I got through it with courage and the help of my mother. Even though I was hurt by all the name-calling, I knew they were going to be the ones left behind. Sometimes I snapped back at them but I knew if I kept my mouth shut and kept achieving my goals, no one could stop me.

Now when I see the people that made fun of me I just walk right by them because I'm going somewhere with my life. So if I stop to talk to them I might get trapped up in their mess. I'm a strong-minded person and very opinionated. That is probably why they don't like me but I don't care. I have goals and if I have courage I can do anything I put my mind to. God made me to be who I am so if someone doesn't like me I'm not going to cry or get upset. I'm like a mountain that can't be moved because I'm proud of myself and what I've accomplished in my life even though my life just started.

You know how people say that "Sticks and stones may break your bones but words will never hurt?" That is a fib because words really do hurt if they are used in a bad way.

Now I can go to my mother and talk to her about a lot of different things. Now when kids call me names I know that they don't have enough love in their home so they make everyone else miserable. I think that everybody should have courage in order to move forward. I noticed the name-calling when I got to middle school, but I knew that I had to be strong. My inner voice told me not to stop to talk, but to keep reaching my goal. My mother always told me that they are your friends today, but your enemies tomorrow. I have only two friends that I still talk to today. It is not hard to find courage if you believe in yourself. When you start to see courage then you can see the light when you know when you have reached the end.

A lot of my teachers have helped me get through a lot. They are Ms. Hinds, Ms. Brown, and Ms. Gooding. These teachers also have a lot of courage in their lives. When I hear kids mocking me I walk right by them and leave them in the dust. I know when I get to the end that only one person is going to be waiting for me and that is my mother.

When kids mock you walk right by them because their words are going to make you a stronger person and will keep you on the road to success. Remember that God didn't make everyone special and that you are yourself and there isn't anybody that can tell you anything else. People might talk about you, but don't let it put you down. Remember that you are not the only one that is made fun of. We all are special in our own way. You think that your friends are your friends but they are the ones that talk the most about you. Don't let their words put you down. Keep your head up high and tell yourself that you are somebody. There is always someone that you can talk to. Never fight them back physically but fight back with courage and you will get farther than you ever thought that you could.

The Courage of Boston's Children, Volume XV, The Max Warburg Courage Curriculum, Inc. and the Boston Public Schools, Houghton Mifflin, 2006.

SAMANTHA

Courage in My Life

Do you know how it feels to be made fun of? Well I do. A lot of times people talk about me. They are always talking about how big I am. When people talk about me, my feelings get hurt and it makes me feel like nobody wants to be my friend. Sometimes I wish I could be as skinny as them, but I don't think it should matter how big someone is. What should matter is your personality and how you treat others. People call me names like "fatty" and I just ignore them. I think people call me names because they might think I'm different.

I think that the kids that call me names are not going to have a good job when they grow up because they always say mean words to me or to other students. I think the kids that get called names like me must feel the same way as I do. Sometimes I wish people could not be overweight so that nobody would have to get called names.

When I come home and I tell my mom or step dad that somebody called me a name they make me feel better. I always say to myself that I am going to lose weight so I won't get made fun of. My mom and step dad say, "Don't listen to the people that call you names because it isn't true."

I feel like wherever I go kids call me names, and I don't like that because it makes me embarrassed, and then everyone looks at me. I try not to eat a lot because sometimes when I eat I think I gain weight. I also try not to eat a lot so people or kids won't say, "Oh, you gained weight." I think that the people that are skinny don't know how big people feel when they call them mean names.

I am courageous because I do not say anything back to the people who call me names. I just ignore them and tell myself not to listen to them. I choose to show courage by not listening to these people because what they say is not true. It shouldn't matter how big you are. The most important thing is how you treat people. I think that I show a lot of courage when people call me names.

The Courage of Boston's Children, Volume XV, The Max Warburg Courage Curriculum, Inc. and the Boston Public Schools, Houghton Mifflin Company, 2006.

Courage in My Life

It was my cousin, Flamo's first time in the United States, and therefore, his first time attending an American school. Because it was the middle of the school year, I thought he would be a bit nervous. I knew it would be hard for him to make friends because he didn't speak much English, and had a strong accent. I also figured most of the kids already knew each other, and it is hard to "break in" halfway through the year.

My family moved to America, at the same time, during my second grade year. I, too, knew little English, and making friends was quite a challenge. I felt very left out. Because of my own experience, I thought I should help him with any problems so he would not feel left out like I did.

If he was anything like me, I was pretty sure Flamo would not sleep well the night before he started attending an American school. He also woke up early the morning school was to start. We ate breakfast, and off we went.

When he came back from school, I asked him if he had a good time. He said, "Yes."

Because that was not what I expected, I was surprised to hear this answer, I asked what happened. He said, "All we did was go over the rules and then I sat all by myself." I asked him. if this was different, for him, than being a student in Africa.

He told me, "In Africa I was one of the smartest kids in my class. I always had a lot of fun in school." The next day he went back to school. When he returned home, I asked him the same questions that I had asked the day before. This time, however, Flamo responded with, "I had a rough day."

When I asked him why it was such a rough day, he said, "When the teacher called my name, most of the kids started laughing. The teacher asked them what was so funny. They said, 'We are laughing at his name.' Also when I raised my hand to give an answer they all started to laugh."

I gave him this advice, "Act like you're not hearing them because they are trying to make you not raise your hand and that will make you get a bad grade. When you have the right answer you should always raise your hand. If they keep laughing, don't give up, tell the teacher."

Flamo asked, "You seem like you understand. Did the same thing happen to you?"

I said, "Yes, in the second grade, and I did the same thing I am telling you to do. I never gave up and didn't allow anyone's silly comments to keep me from participating and learning."

"Do you have any homework to do?" I asked.

"Yes:' he said. "I know what to do but don't get what the question is asking." He asked me to read it. When I was done reading and explaining, Flamo said, "Now I get it! You are the best cousin I have ever had!" Hearing this, I felt so proud, knowing I was able to help my cousin overcome this challenge.

A few weeks later my cousin told me, "Now I am making friends. And I feel happy. Thank you."

The Courage of Boston's Children, Volume XVI, The Max Warburg Courage Curriculum, Inc. and the Boston Public Schools, Houghton Mifflin Company, 2007.

TSEGA

Courage in My Life

In 2005, at the James W. Hennigan School, I was a 5th grader. One day in class we got our math test scores back and a girl named Kalsang had a better score than anyone. A boy in my class was not happy that she got the best score. So he told me and all of his other friends that he had a plan to do something about it.

At lunch time he was going to hit her with a milk box that had milk in it so that everyone could laugh at her. I felt something inside. He was taking it too far.

I realized that I became friends with him because I wanted to hang out with the cool kids, but this was something I could not let him do, even if I had to give up hanging out with the cool kids. So, at lunch time, instead of being with my friends, I followed Kalsang everywhere. He could not do it at lunch because of the lunch mothers, so he told everyone that he would do it at recess.

I did not stop following her. I went everywhere she went. She told me, "Go away! You're the same as them!"

I was just like them until then. Who could blame her for her response? When we got outside, he was hiding somewhere so I was looking everywhere for him. After about 5 minutes it was time to line up and there were people everywhere, so he took advantage of that and threw the box. I knew he was going to, so I jumped in front of her and took the hit. Everyone was laughing at me. I know I did the right thing even though I lost my so-called friends.

After that day they always called me names and said that she was my girlfriend. I ignored all that. Because of this incident, I learned how to make real friends—the type who know what is good. These are the real cool kids. I was also happy because some of the good kids got to know the real me, the one who is nice and kind, not the one who does things that are crazy just to be cool.

The Courage of Boston's Children, Volume XVI, The Max Warburg Courage Curriculum, Inc. and the Boston Public Schools, Houghton Mifflin Company, 2007.

SHELLY

Courage in My Life

Courage. Courage to me means showing bravery, even if you are scared. My memories will tell you how I showed courage. In 2001, this little girl started third grade here at the Richard J. Murphy School. That little girl was me. Older kids that went to this school always bothered me, even some kids that are the same age as me. Those kids bothered me, agitated me, and called me names like "Scarface" and "Burnt eyes." It happened every time I tried to walk by or just happened to ramble past them. They made fun of how I was dressed and what my religion was. When I got home from school every day, my eyes were full of tears. I felt just like a teddy bear in a burning building, waiting to be rescued.

For two years, it kept on happening. Kids threw rocks and dirt at me when I walked home. They also spit on me on the bus when I was not looking. Older kids threatened me to give them my leftover lunch money from school. Whenever these things happened, the other kids would stand there and laugh at me, even the friends that came from the Holland school. You wouldn't feel good if you were hurt, crying to yourself, while the other kids laugh at you.

I always told people that my day at school was great. But it really wasn't. On January 13, 2005, that little girl finally did something. I had to tell someone whom everyone trusts. I told a sixth grade teacher, Ms. Dahill. She knew it hurt my feelings a lot so she sent me to Mrs. Lopes, the sixth, seventh, and eighth grades principal. She told me to go to Mrs. Carrigan, the assistant Principal. I experienced racism throughout all the schools I went to. All those years helped me learn something. If you know someone is being bothered by or being hurt, tell a teacher or an adult that you can trust to help that person. If someone is bothering you, tell someone or try to stop it. I learned this because all those years, I never said anything to anyone when they were threatening me. Now I know that I did make a difference, and I did show courage in my life.

In conclusion, I encouraged myself when no one helped me. I stopped it when people bothered me. After that day, I thought to myself, "Am I brave, or am I a coward?" I'm brave and I showed how I was brave. For once, I did something right, I did something to help myself, I showed courage in my life.

The Courage of Boston's Children, Volume XIV, The Max Warburg Courage Curriculum, Inc. and the Boston Public Schools, Houghton Mifflin Company, 2005.

Stories on Bullying

How Beetle Got Her Colors by Elisa Pearmain
A wise Parrot teaches a bullying Rat a lesson.

Feathers by Elisa Pearmain
A Rabbi teaches a gossip a lesson.

Hanukkah Lights by Carol Wintle
A community lights up against hatred.

HOW BEETLE GOT HER COLORS

by Elisa Pearmain

Long ago in the Amazon rain forest, there lived a common brown rat. A rat who talked like she was all that! She talked loud, she drew a crowd. She teased, and poked, she made rude jokes. "You call yourself a frog, I call you bump on a log!"

Some animals thought she was cool, but it looked more like cruel. One day, for example, she came upon Turtle ambling down the path towards the river. "Hey, moving house, the minimum speed limit's five miles per hour!" When Turtle didn't move fast enough, she flipped him off the road, and he lay on his back, his legs flailing.

Or if Mouse was going by with dinner in his hand, she'd say, "I'll take that, and don't say nothin', or they'll find your head over my fireplace, full of stuffing."

When someone starts bullying, those who don't want to get teased do one of two things: they either get as far away as they can, or as close as they can-both ways hoping to avoid abuse. Well pretty soon, some of the other animals were vying for Rat's attention. "I'm vice-rat of this gang. Hey, I'm her spokesrat!"

Rat loved the attention. She soaked it up. But secretly she wished that she were not a rat at all, but something much bigger, say a cat or a leopard. Yes, a leopard, with spots, or a jet-black panther. And lose the pointy nose; she wanted a snub nose and night vision. Oh man, she would be the queen of the jungle!

But every morning when she woke up and looked into the reflecting pool, she was still a brown rat, and so she just kept on tormenting the smaller animals. Her gang followed behind, laughing at her jokes and helping in her antics.

Now one day, Rat and her gang spied a little brown beetle coming down the path. "Well, what do we have here?" Rat said, laughing. "A little brown tank with sticks for legs. Hey if you rub those stick legs together, can you get fire?"

"Rat-a-tat!" Rat's gang laughed. "Oh, but look, your hard back is so shiny, I can see myself in it. Don't look too bad today," she said, looking away quickly. She felt that old feeling of wishing that she were bigger, with a glossy coat and spots! This made her mad, so she threw Beetle aside like a Frisbee.

Now in that part of the rain forest, there lived a wise and magical parrot that had been listening to Rat for long enough. He knew that inside every big shot, things are not so hot. Parrot flew down and helped Beetle to get right side up again.

"Rat, I am sick of your mean titter tat!" he said. "Why don't we have a contest and settle things once and for all? Whoever wins will get to choose a new coat of any color or texture. Whoever loses will be more respectful of the other animals. I will decide the contest. You shall race from this tree to the big kapok tree on the other side of the forest."

Rat could hardly believe her ears: a new coat! Her prayers were going to be answered! Yes, she could see it now—even if she wasn't as big, she would be the most beautiful rat this side of the rain forest. Why even the big animals would respect her.

"Yeah, a race. Are you ready, little bug? Better do some deep stick bends-hah! Too bad you can't lose the tank. It sure will slow you down!"

Rat began to stretch her massive calf and thigh muscles. Beetle loosened up her shoulder muscles and closed her eyes.

"Are you ready, little Beetle?" Parrot asked.

"Yes, oh wise one," Beetle answered.

"Are you ready, Rat?"

"Am I ready? I'm not even going to get sweaty! Let's go..."

156

Empowering Children to Help Stop Bullying at School

"On my signal." Then the parrot gave the cry, "Go!"

Off went Rat. She turned and looked back. "I don't even see that little tank, left in the dust. Hey, if it sits too long, it just might rust. This is sort of like that tortoise and the hare thing, only I ain't stupid enough to go to sleep. But I can dream a little."

Rat ran along, fantasizing about how she was going to look. "Jet-black furor spots? Hey, I don't have to decide! I can have jet-black fur, and one spot right in the middle of my face. Take the emphasis off the shnoz."

Rat was coming up to the finish line and looked back. "Still no sign of the tick! Here I come! Everyone is cheering, and I can hear them. Here I come. I'll give it a little spurt. Hey, why aren't they looking at me? Huh?"

There was Beetle, sitting on the other side of the finish line, doing a delicate bow.

"You didn't pass me. How'd you get here?" Rat shouted.

"I flew," Beetle said quietly.

"I didn't know you could fly."

Parrot flew to a branch just above the ground. "There's a lot you don't know about Beetle, or any of the other animals that you tease, Rat," said Parrot. "All animals have special gifts. But you don't know about them, because you don't ask. You give them a two-second look and make a lifetime judgment."

"And now, dear Beetle, what would you like for a coat?" asked Parrot.

"I will keep my hard shell, for it helps me to fly and offers protection, but I would like some colors, please. Blue, like the sky, and green like the trees—and could they be shining and shimmering, like the water?"

"Your wish is granted," said Parrot, spreading his wings.

That is why to this day, one species of beetle in the rain forest is a beautiful shimmering blue-green. It's also why rats look pretty much as they always have, though they don't pick on others so much. They mind their own business, making the best of their gifts like everyone else, scurrying around the jungle floor.

Once Upon a Time... Storytelling to Teach Character and Prevent Bullying: Lessons from 99 Multicultural Folk Tales for Grades K-8, Character Development Group, Inc., 2006.

FEATHERS

Long ago in Poland, in a little Jewish village, the people loved their Rabbi. The Rabbi was the most important person in the village because he took care of the people in so many ways. The Rabbi officiated over Temple services and religious holidays. He was also the town judge, and everyone took his or her conflicts to him. He was also the counselor, listening to people's pain and offering clever advice.

One year in this village, the Rabbi noticed that many villagers were coming to him with the same complaint about a man in the village named Chaim. "Chaim is a gossip," the people told the Rabbi. "He is spreading stories that hurt us!"

"He's mean," others said. "His sharp tongue cuts like a knife!"

One woman came to the Rabbi in a frenzy. "Rabbi," she said, "Chaim spread a story that he saw me talking to a strange man in the marketplace. I was only giving directions. Now my husband is angry with me."

The baker said, "Rabbi, when Chaim came for his bread the other day, I gave him the wrong change by mistake. Now he is telling everyone that I am a cheat, and my business is off!"

Another woman came to the Rabbi. "Rabbi, you know I've had a bad back since my fall three years ago. Chaim says I'm a fake, and that my back isn't really bad. He told my friends that he saw me dancing in my living room."

On and on, the complaints came, until the Rabbi decided that he had to take action. He called Chaim to his home. "Chaim," he said, "many people are coming to me, saying that you've been telling stories about them that aren't true and speaking badly of them. Chaim, you are hurting your fellow villagers with your words."

"Oh Rabbi," said Chaim, bowing his head. "I'm sorry. I didn't mean any harm. They are only words. I'll go and take them back and apologize. Everything will be all right after that."

"It's not so simple, Chaim. Once you start your stories, you cannot take them back," the Rabbi said.

"Oh sure I can, Rabbi, you'll see," Chaim repeated.

"Chaim," the Rabbi sighed, "I need to teach you something. Tomorrow morning, come to the Village Square and bring your best feather pillow."

Chaim agreed and went home, thinking that he had not gotten off badly with the loss of one feather pillow.

The next day Chaim met the Rabbi in the Town Square. The Rabbi had a pair of scissors in his hands. He took Chaim's pillow and cut open the top. "Chaim," he said. "I want you to take all of the feathers out of the pillow and throw them into the air." Chaim looked at the Rabbi and then began to take he feathers out of the pillow and to throw them into the air. *Some of them* fell to the ground. Others caught the wind and flew up into the sky, catching on the trees and the rooftops. Some flew away altogether.

When all of the feathers were gone from the pillow, the Rabbi made another request. "Now, Chaim, I want you to put all of the feathers back in the pillow."

Chaim looked at the Rabbi as if he were crazy. "Rabbi, that's not so simple!" Chaim complained. "How could I get all of the feathers back? They have gone everywhere, up in the trees, the rooftops, and some have gone away completely. I would never be able to find them."

"You are right, Chaim," the Rabbi said, smiling. "And your gossip-ing words are just like those feathers. Once you say them, you cannot control where they go or whom they hurt, and you certainly cannot take them back. Do you understand, Chaim?"

"Yes, Rabbi." Chaim hung his head. "I will not gossip again."

Chaim went home and tried his best not to speak unkindly or untruthfully against others. Just to be sure that he remembered the lesson, the Rabbi nailed a feather to Chaim's front door.

Once Upon a Time... Storytelling to Teach Character and Prevent Bullying: Lessons from 99 Multicultural Folk Tales for Grades K-8, Character Development Group, Inc., 2006.

HANUKKAH LIGHTS

by Carol Wintle

In 1996 the Markovitz family was one of a few Jewish families in the suburban neighborhood of Newtown, Pennsylvania. It was Christmas and homes on their street were lit up with decorations of reindeer, wreaths, and Nativity scenes. It was also Hanukkah, so in the front window of the Markovitz home was an electric Menorah, with bulbs that looked like candles.

At sundown, on the first night of Hanukkah, the Markovitzes turned on the first two bulbs. On the second night they lit three bulbs and on the third night they lit four.

The next day, sometime before dawn, the shattering of glass awakened Mrs. Markovitz. Someone had broken their front window, grabbed the Menorah, and smashed it, breaking all nine bulbs.

"My husband and I ran downstairs," Mrs. Markovitz said, "and saw the Menorah was on the floor. The frame was shattered. They must have used a bat. Whoever did it had to squeeze behind bushes to reach it." The family was devastated and afraid.

"We were home much of that day," said Mrs. Markovitz, "because my husband had to get the window replaced. Neighbors kept approaching us to say how sorry they were."

No one knew whom the vandal or vandals were, but it was obvious that the Markovitz home had been singled out for attack.

After the workmen repaired the window, the Markovitzes went to a relative's home for the rest of the day.

Meanwhile their neighbor Margie Alexander told her family, "I have to do something. I'm going to get a Menorah. I don't know if it is going to help, but maybe it will if there is more than one family to target."

Margie found the only Menorah left in their town and put it in the front window of her home. She called Lisa Keeling, another neighbor, and the two of them launched a plan. Margie would call more neighbors. Lisa would drive to other suburbs and look for Menorahs.

When the Markovitz family returned home that evening they saw Menorah bulbs burning in the windows of twenty-five Christian homes. The neighbors had bought a new Menorah for the Markovitzes as well. No longer afraid, the Markovitzes placed the Menorah in their front window and turned on five of the bulbs. Mrs. Markovitz told her children that she felt sorry for the vandals that had broken their Menorah bulbs. "To get up early to do such a thing, they must have had a lot of hatred," she said. "This is what Hanukkah is about, the freedom to do what we want and to fight evil. Right here in our neighborhood was a show of force against hate. And we beat the evil."

Vicky Markovitz, Judy's daughter, remembers that time as an example of compassion and community. Years later she told a reporter, "It was as if they said, if you break their windows, you will have to break ours."

Empowering Children to Help Stop Bullying at School

Resources

Beane, Allan. *The Bully Free Classroom, Over 100 Tips and Strategies for Teachers K-8.* Free Spirit Publishing, 1999.

A helpful bullying prevention curriculum for K-8 schools.

Borba, Michelle. *Nobody Likes Me, Everybody Hates Me, The Top 25 Friendship Problems and How to Solve Them.* Jossey-Bass, 2005.

A guide for parents and teachers of children ages 4-15. It shows how to help young people develop the friendship-building skills they need to make and keep friends, and deal with peer pressure. Contains sections titled: Bullied and Harassed, Teased, and Cliques.

Brown, Lyn Mikel. *Girlfighting: Betryayal and Rejection among Girls,* New York University Press, 2003.

A well researched exploration into what causes some girls to be mean to other girls and what adults can do about it.

Coloroso, Barbara. *The Bully, the Bullied, and the Bystander: From Preschool to High School— How parents and teachers can help break the cycle of violence,* Harper Collins, 2004.

The author of this book describes the bully, the bullied and the bystander as "three characters in a tragic play" where "the scripts can be rewritten, new roles created and the plot changed."

Davis, Stan and Julia. *Schools Where Everyone Belongs: Practical Strategies for Reducing Bullying.* Research Press, 2005.

This book provides practical information for school personnel and parents on how to use a Dan Olweus-type school-wide Bullying Prevention Program to reduce bullying at school.

Davis, Stan and Julia. *Empowering Bystanders In Bullying Prevention,* Research Press, 2007.

The authors describe their unique way to educate students in grades K-8 about bullying and what bystanders can do.

Dellasega, Cheryl. *Girl Wars: Strategies That Will End Female Bullying.* Simon & Shuster, 2003.

This text discusses how to help girls who are targets and witnesses of bullying. It includes information on relational aggression and cyber-bullying.

Dubin, Nick. *Asperger syndrome and bullying: strategies and solutions.* Jessica Kingsley Publishers, 2007.

This resource describes how children on the autism spectrum are often easy targets of bullying. It explores ways to empower children who are bullied, silent witnesses, teachers, parents and schools, and understand children who bully.

Espelage, Dorothy and Swearer, Susan. *Bullying in American Schools: A Social-Ecological Perspective on Prevention and Intervention,* Lawrence Erlbaum Associates, 2004.

This text presents a well-researched systems approach to understanding the causes of bullying and methods for prevention and intervention.

Freedman, Judy. *Easing the Teasing: Helping Your Child Cope with Name-Calling, Ridicule, and Verbal Bullying.* Contemporary Books, 2002.

This guide provides information on why children tease each other, ten strategies for dealing with teasers, and how parents and teachers can help.

Garbarino, James. *And words can hurt forever: how to protect adolescents from bullying, harassment, and emotional violence*, Free Press, 2002.

This book analyzes the many faces of bullying, issues of power and groups, and the secret life of adolescents. The author reflects on the concept of emotionally safe schools.

Garrett, Anne, *Keeping American Schools Safe: A Handbook for Parents, Students, Educators, Law Enforcement Personnel and the Community*. McFarland & Company, Inc., 2001.

This publication presents information on children who act aggressively, effective violence prevention programs in the U.S., and suggestions on what parents and communities can do to reduce community crime and keep schools safe.

Garrity, C., Jens, K., Porter, W., Sager, N. and Short-Camilli, C. *Bully-proofing your school: A comprehensive approach for elementary schools*, Sopris West, 2000.

This curriculum guide provides a whole-school approach for elementary schools.

Heinrichs, Rebekah. *Perfect Targets: Asperger Syndrome and Bullying, Practical Solutions for Surviving the Social World*, Autism Asperger Publishing Company, 2003.

This guide presents a whole school bullying prevention approach that reflects an understanding and sensitivity to the unique needs of students with Asperger Syndrome. It contains an excellent "Modified Inventory of Wrongful Activities," which can be used to survey students to determine the extent of bullying occurring in a school.

Kowalski, Robin, Limber, Susan, Agatston, Patricia. *Cyber Bullying: Bullying in the Digital Age*, Blackwell Publishing, 2008.

This book contains a thorough summary of information on traditional as well as cyber bullying.

McCoy, Elin. *What to Do: When Kids Are Mean To Your Child*. Readers Digest, 1997.

This comprehensive manual offers advice for parents on how to help their children deal with disrespect.

Middleton-Moz, Jane and Zawadski, Mary Lee. *Bullies: From the Playground to the Boardroom, Strategies for Survival*. Health Communications Inc., 2002.

In this book, in-depth case studies of bullying from childhood to adulthood are explored with descriptions of ways adults can help a child stop bullying.

Newman, Katherine S. Rampage: *The Social Roots of School Shootings*. Basic Books, 2004.

This text offers detailed research and analysis on school shootings and discusses the connection between school shootings and various social issues including bullying.

Olweus, Dan. *What we know and what we can do*. Blackwell, 1993.

This is the original summary of Dan Olweus's research on bullying and bullying prevention.

Olweus, Dan and Limber, Sue. *Blueprints for Violence Prevention—Book Nine: Bullying Prevention Program*. Center for the Study and Prevention of Violence, 1999.

The Blueprints for Violence Prevention series are summations of programs that meet very high scientific standards for being effective prevention programs and are recommended for replication in the United States.

Olweus, D., Limber, S., Flerx, V. C., Mullin, N., Riese, J. and Snyder, M., Olweus. *Bullying Prevention Program: Schoolwide guide*, Hazelden, 2007.

This guide is an up-to-date presentation of the whole-school *Olweus Bullying Prevention Program*.

Empowering Children to Help Stop Bullying at School

Pearmain, Elisa Davy. *Once Upon a Time... Storytelling to Teach Character and Prevent Bullying: Lessons from 99 Multicultural Folk Tales for Grades K-8*, Character Development Group, Inc., 2006.

This collection of entertaining stories for children in grades K-8 is paired with a wealth of classroom activities. It is designed to enhance development of character with chapters on courage, empathy, friendship, leadership, respect, responsibility, self-control and bullying prevention.

Prothrow-Stith, Deborah and Spivak, Howard. *Sugar & Spice and No Longer Nice: How we can stop girls' violence*, Jossey-Bass, 2005.

This well-researched text helps adults understand how violent girls have become and how to prevent the escalation of this problem.

Rivers, I., Duncan, N., and Besag, V. *Bullying: A Handbook for Educators and Parents*, Praeger, 2007.

This book provides a review of research on bullying behavior and the long-term effects of bullying. It discusses the challenges that parents of special needs students face and how they can engage proactively with school staff to help stop bullying.

Ross, Dorothea, *Childhood Bullying and Teasing*, American Counseling Association, 1996.

This guide provides an overview of bullying and teasing with theories and practical solutions for parents and school staff.

Sanders, Cheryl and Phye, Gary. *Bullying: Implications for the Classroom*, Elsevier Academic Press, 2004.

This text summarizes international research in education, social, developmental, and counseling psychology. It examines the personality and background of those who bully and are bullied and how families, peers, and schools influence bullying behavior. Intervention techniques are discussed.

Sheras, Peter with Sherill Tippins, *Your Child: Bully or Victim? Understanding and Ending Schoolyard Tyranny*, Skylight Press, 2002.

This book presents information on how parents can help children who are bullied or who silently watch.

Simons, Rachel. *Odd Girl Out: The Hidden Culture of Aggression in Girls*, Boys Town Press, 2002.

This expose explores the world of girl bullying and its relationship to issues of popularity, cliques, jealousies, and competition. Comparisons are made to bullying by males.

Thompson, Michael, Cohen, Lawrence, and Grace, Catherine O'Neill. *Mom, They're Teasing Me: Helping Your Child Solve Social Problems*, Ballantine Books, 2002.

This source book offers parents advise on how to help children handle teasing and bullying.

Wiseman, Rosalind. *Queen Bees & Wannabes: Helping your daughter survive cliques, gossip, boyfriends and other realities of adolescence*, Crown Publishers, 2002.

This book explores the concept of relational bullying, the kind girls most often use, and presents analysis, and helpful suggestions.

Children's Nonfiction Books on Bullying

Brequet, Teri. *Frequently Asked Questions about Cyberbullying*, Rosen Publishing, 2007.

This book, written for teenagers covers such topics as: What is cyberbullying?, Who are cyberbullies and their victims? and What to do if you're being cyberbullied.

Brown, Laurie Krasny and Marc. *How to be a friend*, Little Brown and Company, 1998.

This light-hearted picture book covers topics such as: ways to be a friend and ways not to be a friend, shyness, bosses and bullies, talking out an argument and making up.

Carlson, Nancy. *How to Lose All Your Friends*, Puffin Books, 1997.

Through humor and reverse psychology, the author shows children how to lose all their friends by never smiling or sharing, being a bully and poor sport, tattling and whining.

Cooper, Scott. *Speak Up and Get Along! Learn the Mighty Might, Thought Chop, and more tools to make friends, stop teasing, and feel good about yourself*, Free Spirit Publishing, 2005.

This self-help guide contains many examples of how to assertively resolve a small conflict, tell others what you think, get what you need, end teasing, and start a conversation.

Criswell, Patti Kelley. *a smart girl's guide to friendship troubles: dealing with fights, being left out & the whole popularity thing*, American Girl Library, Pleasant Company Publications, 2003.

Topics and good advice presented in this resource include what to do about: getting left out, when and how to speak up, on-again/off-again friends, back-stabbers, toxic friendships, when friends are cruel to others, cleaver comebacks, and communicating with adults.

Criswell, Patti Kelley, *Stand Up for Yourself & Your Friends: Dealing with Bullies and Bossiness, and Finding a Better Way*, American Girl Publishing Inc., 2009.

An excellent guidebook for girls on how to stand up for yourself and others.

Finn, Carrie. *Kids Talk about Bullying*. Picture Window Books, 2007.

In this picture book, fifth grader Super Sam the Problem-solver gives peers advice on how to deal with bullying.

Kalman, Izzy. *Bullies to Buddies,* The Wisdom Pages, 2005.

This self-help guide encourages the use of "cool" rather than "erupting" responses to bullying. It is important to note that the author places responsibility for stopping bullying on the children who are bullied. He discourages peers from helping students who are bullied or communicating with teachers unless physical harm is involved.

Kaufman, G and Raphael, L. *Stick up for yourself: Every Kid's Guide to Personal Power and Positive Self-Esteem*, Free Spirit Publishing, 1990.

This is a children's guidebook on how to feel better about yourself, be more confident and assertive, and understand and manage how you feel.

Levete, Sarah. *"Let's Talk About" Keeping Safe.* Stargazer Books, 2007.

This picture book focuses on safety over-all and provides many good suggestions related to dealing with bullying.

Empowering Children to Help Stop Bullying at School

Lewis, Barbara A. *What Do You Stand For? A Kid's Guide to Building Character*, Free Spirit Press, 1998.

This is a children's handbook on how to become the type of person who makes friends easily and others look up to. It provides true stories, challenging dilemmas and activities on how to become more courageous, caring, imaginative, peaceful and responsible.

McGraw, Jay. *Jay McGraw's Life Strategies for Dealing with Bullies,* Aladdin, 2008.

This self-help book reinforces the concepts presented in *Empowering Children to Help Stop Bullying at School.*

Romaine, Trevor. *Bullies are a Pain in the Brain,* Free Spirit Publishing, 1997.

This non-fiction book provides helpful advice in a humorous way.

Romaine, Trevor. *Cliques, Phonies & Other Baloney.* Free Spirit Press, 1998.

In this book helpful suggestions are made with humor. Young people are shown they can handle social difficulties while remaining true to who they really are.

Simons, Rachel. *Odd Girl Speaks Out,* Harcourt, 2003.

This is the sequel to *Odd Girl Out.* Teenage girls write poems, songs, confessions, stories, and essays about their personal experiences with bullying, back-stabbing, female cruelty and their visions for change.

Thomas, Pat. *Stop Picking on Me: A First Look at Bullying,* Barron's Educational Series, 2000.

This picture book shows that it is normal to be afraid and worried when you are bullied.